The
Doctrine
of
ANGELS
&DEMONS

**Guide to
Bible Doctrine**

The
Doctrine
of
ANGELS
&DEMONS

Norman L. Geisler
Douglas E. Potter

Indian Trail, North Carolina

The Doctrine of Angels and Demons
NGIM Guide to Bible Doctrine, Volume 5
Norman L. Geisler and Douglas E. Potter

Copyright © 2016 Norman L. Geisler.

Published by Norm Geisler International Ministries | P.O. Box 2638 |
Indian Trail,
NC 28079 | USA
www.ngim.org

Printed in the United States of America

ISBN–13: 978-1539852018
ISBN–10: 1539852016

Contents

**Norm Geisler International Ministries
Guide to Bible Doctrine**

www.NGIM.org

Introduction

Scripture everywhere assumes the reality and activity of angels. They are at the beginning when God banished the first human couple from the Garden of Eden and "stationed the cherubim and the flaming sword which turned every direction to guard the way to the tree of life" (Gen. 4:24) to the very end when Jesus sends His angel "to testify to you these things for the churches . . ." (Rev. 22:16). Such a study, therefore, is important to the Christian faith.

Long technical treaties on this doctrine while important, can be intimidating to the Christian that wants to dig into the study for the first time. Even some less technical approaches might not state the doctrine in as systematic or comprehensive manner as it should. As a result, those new to the study of this doctrine may never be exposed to important concepts and issues.

Christians, more than ever, need a study of angelic creatures that is true and systematic. Many in and outside the church do not understand how this doctrine is formulated, how it intersects and informs many areas of Christian thought and life which serves as a foundation to a Christian worldview.

This book is a popular introduction to the study of angels and demons (angelology and demonology) firmly rooted in the evangelical tradition. Each chapter covers an area of the doctrine, stresses its basis, doctrinal importance and interconnectedness to formulating a Christian view of angels, demons and other doctrines. The study questions provided help reinforce the material and make it usable even for a formal study of angels. It is ideal for personal study or in groups for the home, church, school or ministry environment.

The approach is faithful to the historical evangelical position that integrates all truth as God's truth and upholds the classical view of the full inspiration and inerrancy of the Bible.

Dr. Norman L. Geisler has taught theology and Bible doctrine in churches, colleges, and seminaries for over 60 years. Having authored over one hundred works in Christian apologetics and theology (see *Systematic Theology In One Volume*), this work, while maintaining the precision and comprehensiveness the study needs, uniquely makes it accessible to everyone.

Dr. Douglas E. Potter is an assistant professor and Director of the Doctor of Ministry program at Southern Evangelical Seminary. He has been teaching Christian theology and apologetics for over a decade and is an author or co–author of several books.

1

Angels

*Are they not all ministering spirits sent out to serve for
the sake of those who are to inherit salvation.*
Hebrews 1:14

God created spiritual creatures, many of whom are
called angels. Evil angels are called demons, the chief
one being Satan. There is a hierarchy of beings that range
from God to angels to human beings to animals to inanimate matter. This chapter investigates the biblical origin,
names, nature, purpose and organization of angels. We
then develop a biblical doctrine or teaching about angels.
Satan and demons are studied in the next chapters.

ORIGIN OF ANGELS

While the biblical term "angel" is a reference to a certain
kind of spiritual creature (namely, "messengers") that God
created, it is commonly used for all such spiritual creatures. However the same term is used for human "messengers" (1 Sam. 6:21; James 2:25) and is even used for the

preincarnate messenger of Yahweh [LORD] who is Christ (see below).

Angels are not eternal since they were created. Only God is eternal. The psalmist declared, "Praise Him, all His angels; Praise Him, all His hosts! . . . Let them praise the name of the Lord, For He commanded and they were created" (Ps. 148:2, 5 cf. Neh. 9:6). Paul says, "For by Him all things were created, both in the heavens and on earth, visible and invisible, whether thrones or dominions or rulers or authorities—all things have been created through Him and for Him" (Col. 1:16). Genesis indicates that they were created at the beginning by God (Gen. 2:1). They were probably created when God created the "heavens and the earth" (Gen. 1:1) and definitely created before the earth, for they sang when its cornerstone was laid (Job 38:6–7).

All angels were created by God through the Son. Paul says,

> For by Him [Jesus Christ] all things were created, both in the heavens and on earth, visible and invisible, whether thrones or dominions or rulers or authorities—all things have been created through Him and for Him. He is before all things, and in Him all things hold together. (Col. 1:16–17)

No creature exists that was not created by Jesus Christ (John 1:1–3). God cannot create an evil creature (see Appendix A): "God saw all that He had made, and behold, it was very good" (Gen. 1:31). "Your eyes are too pure to approve evil" (Hab. 1:13a). Therefore, all angels were originally created holy and completely perfect.

NAMES OF ANGELS

Angels are given different titles and proper names in the Bible. Some of these titles include "angels" ("messengers"– Dan. 4:13), "living creatures" (Rev. 4:6), "angels of God" (John 1:51), "elect angels" (1 Tim. 5:21), "holy angels" (Rev. 14:10), "powerful angels" (2 Thess. 1:7), "chief princes" (Dan. 10:13), "ministers" (Ps. 104:4), "sons of God" (Job 1:6; 2:1), "sons of mighty" (Ps. 89:6; cf. 29:1), "gods" (Heb. 2:7; Ps. 8:5; Gen. 35:7), "holy ones" (Dan. 8:13; Zech. 14:5; Job 15:15), "stars" (Job 38:7; Rev. 12:4), "host" of heaven (Gen. 2:1; Neh. 9:6; Luke 2:13), "chariots" (Ps. 68:17; Zech. 6:5). Some scholars think "elders" in Revelation 4:4 may be angelic beings.

Proper names are given to some angels in the Bible. There is Michael (Dan. 12:1) whose name means "Who is like God?" He is one of the chief princes (Dan. 10:13) and the "archangel" (Jude 9) who disputed with Satan and protects the people of Israel (Dan. 12:1). He is possibly of the cherub class (Ezek. 10:1–13). He is the leader of the heavenly army (Rev. 12:7) and will lead in the final victory over the Devil after the thousand–year reign of Christ (Rev. 12:7). There is Gabriel whose name means "Devoted to God." He "stands in the presence of God" (Luke 1:19). He makes special announcements for God (Luke 1:11–13). He appeared to Mary (Luke 1:26–33) and is a revealer of God's kingdom purposes (Dan. 9:21–22; 8:16). Finally, there is Lucifer (Isa. 14:12) called "son of the morning," who fell and became the Devil. His fallen names are many (see Chapter 2). Presumable, all angels have names. God knows all the stars by number (Isa. 40:26) which are inanimate objects. So God likely has a name for each angel, certainly He knows each one individually since He is all–knowing.

THE NATURE OF ANGELS

Angels are immaterial beings or pure spirits. Their nature is invisible. Colossians 1:16 says, "For by Him all things were created, both in the heavens and on earth, visible and invisible, whether thrones or dominions or rulers or authorities—all things have been created through Him and for Him." Although they have taken on physical forms and appeared to humans (Gen. 18). Hebrews 1:14 calls them "ministering spirits." In Luke 24:39, Jesus said, "A spirit does not have flesh and bones as you see that I have." Many angels can be present in one place (Luke 8:30). Further, it is only by a miracle that mortals can see angels, as when Elisha prayed for the servant to see them: " 'O Lord, I pray, open his eyes that he may see.' And the Lord opened the servant's eyes and he saw; and behold, the mountain was full of horses and chariots of fire all around Elisha" (2 Kings 6:17).

Angels have no Gender

Since they are created finite spirits without bodies, angels have no gender. Hence, they do not engage in marriage or reproduction. Jesus taught, "For in the resurrection they neither marry nor are given in marriage, but are like angels in heaven" (Matt. 22:30).

Some have objected to this based on Genesis 6:1-2, where the "sons of God" (which are angels in Job 1:6; 2:1; 38:7) married the daughters of men. However, there are other interpretations (see Chapter 4). Even if it is a reference to angels, it may be pointing to fallen angels who possessed human beings, who can intermarry.

Angels never Die

Since they have no bodies, angels never die, since they are not subject to decay and death. They are immortal. Luke writes, "but those who are considered worthy to attain to that age and the resurrection from the dead, neither marry nor are given in marriage; for they cannot even die anymore, because they are like angels, and are sons of God, being sons of the resurrection" (Luke 20:35–36). Even rebellious angels are kept in existence and have eternal fire prepared for their punishment (Matt. 25:41).

Angels have Free Will

Angels have free will. This is seen in that some angels willfully rebelled against God therefore face punishment. Jude 6 says, "And angels who did not keep their own domain, but abandoned their proper abode, He has kept in eternal bonds under darkness for the judgment of the great day." Peter says, "For if God did not spare angels when they sinned, but cast them into hell and committed them to pits of darkness, reserved for judgment;" (2 Peter 2:4; cf. 1 Tim. 3:6).

Angels Have Great Intelligence

Angels have great intelligence and wisdom, 2 Samuel 14:20 says, "My lord is wise, like the wisdom of the angel of God, to know all that is in the earth." Such tremendous knowledge is displayed in the Bible (cf. Luke 1:13, Rev. 10:5–6; 17:1). Jesus implied their great but limited knowledge when He said, "But of that day or hour no one knows, not even the angels in heaven, nor the Son, but the Father alone" (Mark 24:31).

Angels Have Great Power

Angels have great power. The messengers sent to Sodom performed a miracle. "They [Angels] struck the men who were at the doorway of the house with blindness, both small and great, so that they wearied themselves trying to find the doorway" (Gen. 19:11). They are called "mighty ones" (Ps. 103:20) and "powerful angels" (2 Thess. 1:7). The ones at Jesus' tomb were able to roll back the heavy stone (Matt. 28:2–3). Speaking of false teachers, Peter says, "Whereas angels who are greater in might and power do not bring a reviling judgment against them before the Lord" (2 Peter 2:11).

Angels are Persons

Angels are persons, since they have intellect, emotions, and will, the three characteristics of persons. They choose to communicate their will with God (Job 1:7), humans (Gen. 18:1f) and each other (Rev. 7:1–3). Emotions or feelings are evidenced in their worship of God (Isa. 6:3; cf. Rev. 4:8–9) and they experience joy upon the repentance of just one sinner (Luke 15:10).

Angels Are Beautiful

Angels are a reflection of God's nature and glory; hence, they are beautiful beings. Isaiah's vision of them in the temple is one of ineffable beauty (Isa. 6:1–7 cf. Ezek. 1:15–16). Daniel had a similar aesthetic experience when an angel appeared to him (Dan. 10:5–6) and the angel at Jesus' tomb "was like lightning, and his clothing as white as snow" (Matt. 28:2–3). Even fallen angels retain the beauty which enhances their ability to deceive (2 Cor. 11:14).

Jesus Christ is Not an Angel

An important distinction to make is between *an* angel of the Lord as a created spiritual being and *the* angel of the Lord as the uncreated Son of God, second person of the Trinity who appears in human form in the Old Testament.

Jesus Christ appears in the Old Testament in His Preincarnate state as "the Angel [Messenger] of the Lord." The term "Yahweh" (Lord) is used exclusively of God in the Old Testament (Isa. 45:18), yet "Yahweh" appeared to the patriarchs" (Ex. 6:2–3). This was done by the

Messenger [Angel] of the Lord who is Yahweh. Exodus 3:2 says, "The angel of the Lord appeared to him [Moses] in a blazing fire from the midst of a bush." The Messenger of the Lord throughout the Old Testament is called God (Gen. 18:1). It is also clear that the Angel of the Lord is a different Person than the Lord. Zechariah 1:12–13 says, "Then the angel of the Lord said, 'O Lord of hosts, how long will You have no compassion for Jerusalem and the cities of Judah, with which You have been indignant these seventy years?' The Lord answered the angel who was speaking . . ." This same kind of conversation takes place in Psalm 110:1, which Jesus used as an argument for His Messiahship against the Pharisees (Matt. 22:42–45).

Hence, *the* Angel of the Lord in the Old Testament serves the same role, as does Christ in the New Testament (Isa. 63:7–10). Once the Son (Christ) came in permanent incarnate form (John 1:1, 14), never again does *the* Angel of the Lord appear. Angels appear, but no angel that is worshiped or claims to be God ever appears again. The Father and Holy Spirit never appear as a man. Hence, Jesus Christ, as a person, eternally existed and appeared as a man before His virginal conception on earth.

Jesus is presented in the New Testament as being fully human, not an angel. He has a human genealogy (Matt. 1:1–17), born of a woman (Matt. 1:18f; Gal. 4:4), He aged (Luke 2:42), increased in knowledge, (Matt. 4:12), prayed (Matt. 14:23), grew hungry (Matt. 4:2), tired (John 4:6), had compassion (Matt. 9:36), wept (John 11:35), grew thirsty (John 19:28) and Jesus is referred to as the "Son of Man" and "Son of David" multiple times. Jesus said, "Foxes have holes and birds of the air have nests, but the Son of Man has no place to lay his head" (Matt. 8:20).

Jesus is also presented in the New Testament as being fully God, not an angel. He is the Creator (John 1:1–3) and sustainer of creation (1 Cor. 8:6). He is Eternal (John 8:58) "I tell you the truth," Jesus answered, "Before Abraham was born, I am!" Which is a clear reference to the Yahweh of the Old Testament (Ex.3:14). In John 17:5 Jesus says, "And now, Father, glorify me in your presence with the glory I had with you before the world began." Jesus is present everywhere (omnipresence) saying, "Go therefore and make disciples of all the nations . . . Teaching them to obey everything I have commanded you. And surely I am with you always, to the very end of the age" (Matt. 28:20). Jesus is all–knowing (omniscience) "He did not need man's testimony about man, for he knew what was in a man" (John 2:25). But Scripture teaches that only God knows what is in a man's heart (1 Kings 8:39). Jesus is all–powerful (omnipotence) "Then Jesus came to them and said, 'All authority in heaven and on earth has been given to me'" (Matt. 28:18). Jesus is un-changeable (Immutable), "Jesus Christ is the same yester-day and today and forever (Heb. 13:8). Jesus performs the works of God as Judge (John 5:21–27) and power to do miracles such as raising the dead (John 11:43). But only God can be and do all of these. Jesus was also worshipped on many occasions (Matt. 28:17; John 9:38; Heb. 1:6), something due to God alone (Matt. 4:10).

Jesus Cannot be Compared to an Angel (Creature)

A significant problem for some today, as well as in the early church, was the confusion of Jesus Christ with the nature of an angel. Hence, Scripture demonstrates that Jesus of Nazareth is God the Son, the second person of the Trinity who took on human flesh. Hence, He is both God and man and therefore the creator of angels. Hence,

He cannot be compared to any angel. John in his Gospel says,

> In the beginning was the Word, and the Word was with God, and the Word was God. He was in the beginning with God. All things came into being through Him, and apart from Him nothing came into being that has come into being. (John 1:1–2)

This verse makes it clear that the Word [Jesus] is the same nature as God and does what only God can do, that is create all things. John continues, "And the Word became flesh, and dwelt among us, and we saw His glory, glory as of the only begotten from the Father, full of grace and truth" (John 1:14). The epistle to the Hebrews perhaps makes the strongest case that Jesus Christ could not be an angel because of His superiority. Hebrews offers several arguments that Jesus could never be or have been an angel. Hebrews 1:1–14 argues that no angel could every qualify for the position and dignity of the Son of God, therefore Jesus being the Son of God could never have been or be an angel.

> God, after He spoke long ago to the fathers in the prophets in many portions and in many ways, in these last days has spoken to us in His Son, whom He appointed heir of all things, through whom also He made the world. And He is the radiance of His glory and the exact representation of His nature, and upholds all things by the word of His power. When He had made purification of sins, He sat down at the right hand of the Majesty on high, having become as much better than the angels, as He has inherited a more excellent name than they. (Heb. 1:1–4)

Hebrews then goes on to list several Old Testament quotations (Ps. 2:7; 2 Sam. 7:14; Ps. 104:4; 45:6–7; 105:25–27; 110:1) to demonstrate that no angel is superior to Jesus Christ as the Son of God (Heb. 1:5–14), given His divine nature. It then shows that no angel is superior to Jesus Christ as the Son of man, given His perfect human nature:

> But we do see Him who was made for a little while lower than the angels, namely, Jesus, because of the suffering of death crowned with glory and honor, so that by the grace of God He might taste death for everyone.
>
> For it was fitting for Him, for whom are all things, and through whom are all things, in bringing many sons to glory, to perfect the author of their salvation through sufferings.
>
> Therefore, since the children share in flesh and blood, He Himself likewise also partook of the same, that through death He might render powerless him who had the power of death, that is, the devil, and might free those who through fear of death were subject to slavery all their lives.
>
> For assuredly He does not give help to angels, but He gives help to the descendant of Abraham. (Heb. 2:9–10; 14–15–16)

Hence, Jesus must be fully God and fully man. No angel could ever be compared to this and therefore Jesus cannot ever have been or be an angel or created being.

Purpose of Angels

Similar to all of God's rational creatures, angels were created for His glory. They sing (Job 38:7) and praise God (Ps. 148:2). Indeed, some angels continually sing "holy, holy, holy" in His presence (Isa. 6:3). Hence, Angels are created to glorify God, "Worthy are You, our Lord and our God, to receive glory and honor and power; for You created all things, and because of Your will they existed, and were created" (Rev. 4:11). They are to serve God since they were created "for Him" (Col. 1:16; cf. Job 1:6; 2:1). Paul says angels desire God's wisdom, "so that the manifold wisdom of God might now be made known through the church to the rulers and the authorities in the heavenly places" (Eph. 3:10; cf. 1 Pet. 1:12). Angels reflect God's attributes. Isaiah majestically records them crying out to one another, "Holy, Holy, Holy, is the Lord of hosts, the whole earth is full of His glory" (Isa. 6:3; cf. Ezek. 1:5, 28). Angels also engage in spiritual warfare in the angelic sphere (Dan. 10:13; 12:1; Isa. 14:4-7; Ezek. 28:12-19) as well as the human sphere (Eph. 6:11-18).

Angels Ministered to Christ

Angels played a significant role in the life of Christ as recorded in the New Testament. The angel Gabriel announced the coming birth of Jesus to Mary (Luke 1:26-28). An angel of the Lord appeared to Joseph in a dream to say, "Joseph, son of David, do not be afraid to take Mary as your wife; for the Child who has been conceived in her is of the Holy Spirit" (Matt. 1:20). An angel of the Lord appeared and spoke to the shepherds watching in the fields on the night of His birth (Luke 2:10-14). Angels ministered to Christ while He was here on earth. After Jesus' temptation, Matthew writes, "Then the devil left Him; and behold, angels came and began to minister to Him (Matt. 4:11; cf. Matt. 26:53; Luke 22:43). Angels announced Jesus' resurrection (Matt. 28:1-6) and appeared at His ascension (Acts 1:9-11). Jesus taught that angels would descend with Him at His Second Coming. Jesus said, "For the Son of Man is going to come in the glory of His Father with His angels, and will then repay every man according to his deeds" (Matt. 16:27; cf. Matt. 25:31; 2

Thess. 1:7). Even in Jesus' glorified and eternal state, angels worship Him. The apostle John writes,

> Then I looked, and I heard the voice of many angels around the throne and the living creatures and the elders; and the number of them was myriads of myriads, and thousands of thousands, saying with a loud voice, "Worthy is the Lamb that was slain to receive power and riches and wisdom and might and honor and glory and blessing." And every created thing which is in heaven and on the earth and under the earth and on the sea, and all things in them, I heard saying, "To Him who sits on the throne, and to the Lamb, be blessing and honor and glory and dominion forever and ever." (Rev. 5:11-14)

Angels Minister to Believers

Angels also minister to believers, God's elect (saved), in multiple of ways. They are involved in communicating God's will and word (Acts 7:52–53; Gal. 3:19). They are involved in some revelation (Matt. 1:20–21), they meet physical needs (Gen 21:17–20; Ps 78:23–25), protection and deliverance (Gen 32:1–32; Rev 7:1–14), strength and encouragement (Acts 5:19–20). They are assigned to watch over children (Matt. 18:10) and many can surround a believer (2 Kings 6:17).

Specifically, they promote evangelism (Acts 8:26), restrain wickedness (Gen. 18:22), announce and execute judgment (Rev. 8, 14, 16, 19). They can be involved in answering prayer (Acts 12:7) and care for believers at the moment of death eventually escorting them into the presence of the Holy One (Luke 16:22).

An important distinction exists between the ministry of angels and that of the Holy Spirit. The Holy Spirit is God (Acts 5:1–4); angels are created by God. Angels may temporally help us, but only the Holy Spirit eternally saves us (Titus 3:5), seals us (2 Cor. 1:22), baptizes us (1 Cor. 12:13), and indwells us (John 14:16). Angels minister *for* us, the Holy Spirit ministers *to* us. Angels *guard* us, the Holy Spirit *guides* us. Angels are *beside* us, the Holy Spirit is *in* us (John 14:16–17).

God explicitly commands humans not to worship angels. Humans and angels worship God alone (Isa. 6:1–4; Rev. 4:6–11; 5:8–14). Indeed, the first commandment states: "I am the Lord your God, . . . "You shall have no other gods before Me" (Ex. 20:1–6). Paul says, "Let no one keep defrauding you of your prize by delighting in self–abasement and the worship of the angels, taking his stand on visions he has seen, inflated without cause by his fleshly mind" (Col. 2:18). The Apostle John was rebuked for worshiping an angel: "I fell down to worship at the feet of the angel . . . But he said to me, 'Do not do that. I am a fellow servant of yours and of your brethren the prophets and of those who heed the words of this book. Worship God' " (Rev. 22:8–9).

Paul states that in our glorified state we will rule with and judge angels: "Or do you not know that the saints will judge the world? If the world is judged by you, are you not competent to constitute the smallest law courts? Do you not know that we will judge angels? How much more matters of this life?" (1 Cor. 6:2–3).

Angels also engage in spiritual warfare. This takes place in the angelic sphere as a battle between good and evil angels, behind the scenes of governments and world events (Dan. 10:13; 12:1; Isa. 14:4–7; Ezek. 28:12–19), as well as the future tribulation period (Rev. 12:7–9). Such spiritual warfare also takes place in the human sphere. Paul says,

> For our struggle is not against flesh and blood,
> but against the rulers, against the powers, against
> the world forces of this darkness, against the
> spiritual forces of wickedness in the heavenly
> places. (Eph. 6:12)

Number and Position of Angels

The number of angels is fixed, not increasing or decreasing (Matt. 22:30), and vast, humanly innumerable (Rev. 5:11). They are described as "hosts" (Ps. 46:7; Luke 2:13) and "myriads" (Deut. 33:2). Angels rank under God and above humans. First Peter 3:22, says of Christ "who is at the right hand of God, having gone into heaven, after angels and authorities and powers had been subjected to Him." Psalm 8:4–5 says, "What is man that You take thought of him, And the son of man that You care for him? Yet You have made him a little lower than God, And You crown him with glory and majesty!" This makes it more amazing that God has chosen believers to judge angels (1 Cor. 6:3).

The most common designation of God's spiritual creatures in the Bible is "angel" meaning "messenger" who are sent on errands to earth. There is rank among both good and evil angels or demons (see Chapter 3). For good angels the top is the archangel (Michael–Dan. 12:1). Under the archangel are "other chief princes" (Dan. 10:21). Cherubim (means "knowledge") are glorious creatures who are proclaimers and protectors of God's glory (Gen. 3:24; Ps. 80:1). Other spiritual beings, called "living creatures," worship God and direct His judgments (Rev. 4:7–8). These may be similar to cherubim, but appear different in Ezekiel 1:6. Seraphim (means "burning ones") are proclaimers of God's holiness (Isa. 6:2–3).

THE ABODE AND ABILITIES OF ANGELS

The general sphere of angels is in heaven. Paul speaks of the third heaven or paradise as being the throne of God. The natural abode of angels is the second heaven. However, they have access to the third heaven (Paradise) and are active there (1 Kings 22:19; Rev. 4:6) as well as on earth (Gen. 28:12; Heb. 1:14). Angels are called before God's throne (Job 1:6, 2:1). Angels can do superhuman things. This may be due to their nature as spirits not having any spatio–temporal limits. Biblically they are depicted as being able to traverse great distances in a short time (Dan. 10:2, 12). They can perform miracles (Gen. 19:1; Rev. 16:14), the can materialize (assume bodily form) even eating food (Gen. 19:3, 18:2, 8). This may be an ability of only some angels since others only appear in visions (not materializing) and evil angels (demons) seek embodiment or possession in other physical beings, apparently not having any way to materialize. Although angels do not have bodies, they may communicate with God (Job 1:7), humans (Gen. 18:1f.) and each other (Rev. 7:1–3). They occupy no space but can relate to beings in space. This is evident in fallen angels (demons) who sometimes possess humans (Luke 8:27–34).

BIBLICAL DOCTRINE OF ANGELS

Angels are lower than God, but higher than human beings. Hence, angels are greater in knowledge and power than humans. Angels are like God, and unlike humans. They have no matter in their being. They are pure spirits while humans are a unity of spirit (soul) and matter. Hence, the only way they can be seen by mortal human beings is by a miracle. Either God must perform a miracle so mortal man can see the spirit world, or He must perform a miracle so that an essentially spirit being can materialize and be seen with mortal eyes.

Angels are not temporal beings, that is, they do not exist in time. Nor are they essentially eternal like God. Hence, they are aeviternal. That is they are by nature not in time, but can relate to time. They are not eternal as only God is, but they can relate to Him. They are what humans will be when they are beatified (Matt. 18:10; Luke 20:35–36). Angels are immortal, since they have no bodies that can die or parts that can be torn asunder. Hence, as simple spirits they are not subject to death (James 2:26).

Each angel is a species of its own. Since they cannot reproduce with their kind, as humans do, they are simple created beings and have no way to divide or multiply (Matt. 22:30). Each is one of a kind. Angels do not change in nature. Their nature is fixed from the moment of their creation. Unlike humans, they do not grow old; they have no age or undergo any kind of change. Also they have no accidents, that is, characteristics not essential to their nature such as size, color, etc. Hence, there is no accidental change. The only kind of change they can undergo is a substantial change such as, creation or annihilation by God.

Since angels cannot change, they are fixed in their nature; hence, once an angel sins, he is doomed forever (2 Peter 2:4; Jude 6). Hence, as the Bible says explicitly Christ did not die to redeem angels (Heb. 2:16). Like all of God's rational and moral creatures, angels were given a choice. And, like humans at death (Heb. 9:27), once they have made their final choice, it is forever too late, and this is something they know (Matt. 8:29).

The difference between God, angels and humans is illustrated in the following chart (Table 1.1).

	GOD	ANGELS	HUMANS
Mode of Being	Uncreated	Created	Created
Limits	Infinite	Finite	Finite
Nature	Spirit	Spirits	Spirit–Body
Simplicity	Absolutely Simple	Relative Simplicity	No Simplicity (A Complex)
Duration	Eternal (Uncreated Eternity)	Aeviternal (Created Everlasting)	Temporal (Created Temporality)
Change	None	None In Nature, Only In Will	Changeable In Nature And Will
Actuality	Pure Actuality	Completed Actuality	Progressively Completed Actuality
Potentiality	None	None Uncompleted	Uncompleted Potentials
Classification (species)	Beyond all classes	Each a class of one	All in one class (a race)
Free will	Unchangeable before and after choice	Changeable before but not after choice	Changeable before and after choice
Redemption	Source Of Redemption	Unredeemable	Redeemable

Table 1.1

Summary

The study of angels shows that God created them as spiritual beings. The physical universe is material; angels are immaterial and human beings are a unity composed of both spirit (soul) and matter. Angels are lower than God and humans are a little lower than the angels. Angels were created to glorify God and minister to God's elect. Their abode is heaven and their abilities far exceed that of humans, yet because of their nature they cannot be redeemed once they freely choose their own destiny, their decision is final.

Questions to Answer

1. What are some important biblical verses on the origin of angels?

2. What are some important biblical verses on the nature of angels?

3. What are some important biblical verses on the purpose of angels?

4. What is the biblical reason Jesus cannot be compared to an angel?

5. How do angels compare to God and man?

2

Satan

Therefore, laying aside falsehood, speak truth each one
of you with his neighbor, for we are members of one
another.
Be angry, and yet do not sin; do not let the sun go down
on your anger and do not give the devil an opportunity.
Ephesians 4:25–27

Although fallen and depraved, Satan is an angel endowed with all their abilities and powers. Our study in this chapter covers Satan's reality, names, personality, depravity and activity.

Satan is identified as an angelic being (Matt. 25:41; Rev. 12:7) and therefore created (Col. 1:15) by God with all the powers endowed to angels (Chapter 1). Indeed, according to Ezekiel (28) Satan is the highest of all created beings and a cherub (Ezek. 28:14).

His Creation

Satan was originally a good spiritual being created by God. "For by Him [Christ] all things were created, in heaven and

27

on earth, visible and invisible . . ." (Col. 1:16). "And without him was not anything made that was made" (John. 1:3). The Psalmist declared, "Praise Him all His angels. . . . For He commanded and they were created" (Ps. 147:2, 5).

His Reality

Evidence for the reality of Satan is both within Scripture and outside of Scripture in the world.

Evidence From Scripture

That Satan is a real being, as opposed to a personification of evil, is affirmed by the Old and New Testaments. Genesis 3:1 says, "Now the serpent was more crafty than any beast of the field which the Lord God had made. And he said to the woman, "Indeed, has God said, 'You shall not eat from any tree of the garden'?" That the serpent was Satan is affirmed by Scripture (Rev. 12:9). Job speaks of Satan having access to the very throng of God "Now there was a day when the sons of God came to present themselves before the Lord, and Satan also came among them" (Job 1:6, cf. 2:1).

Nineteen of the twenty–seven New Testament books refer to Satan (four more to demons). Every writer of the New Testament recognized the reality of Satan. Of the twenty–nine references to Satan in the Gospels, Jesus made twenty–five of them. Jesus had a personal encounter and conversation when He was tempted by Satan, Matthew 4:1, says, "Then Jesus was led up by the Spirit into the wilderness to be tempted by the devil." Hence, Jesus teaches the reality of Satan, in Matthew (4:3–4). Jesus speaks directly to Satan and demons (Luke 8:29–30). Jesus also teaches about Satan's Kingdom (Matt. 12:23–25). Hence, Jesus teaches the personal existence of a being called Satan. He is not merely an idea or per-sonification. Furthermore, Jesus never corrected any one for acknowledging the existence and activity of Satan and demons. This confrontation Jesus and Satan is referred to in Mark 1:12 and Hebrews 4:13. To deny the reality of a personal Satan is to impugn the integrity or sanity of Jesus Christ.

Satan is the enemy of God's people. This is seen from the very beginning of Israel's history, since the Messiah, human salvation, will come through the Jews. Genesis 3:15 says, "And I will put enmity between you and the woman, And between your seed and her seed." This was narrowed to the offspring of Abraham in the Covenant given to him. God assures him and his decedents of His protection: "And I will bless those who bless you, And the one who curses you I will curse" (Gen. 12:1–3; cf. Zech. 3:1). Satan relentlessly attacked that bloodline (Nub. 24:10; Zech. 3:1). The reality of Satan, also entails the reality of Demons since he is their "prince" (Luke 11:15) and their "king" (Rev. 9:11).

Satan being a real angelic being entails he has all the traits of personhood. He has intellect which is described as crafty (2 Cor. 11:3) and is a tempter (Luke 4:11). He is depicted as having the emotions of desire (1 Tim. 3:6), jealousy (Job 1:8, 9), hate (1 Peter 5:8) and anger (Rev. 12:12). All of these emotions are directed towards thwarting the plan and people of God. He has a will in which he gives commands (Luke 4:3, 9) and leads a re-bellion against God and His people (Rev. 20:7–9). He is also held morally responsible for his deception before God. Second Corinthians 11:14–15 says, "Satan disguises himself as an angel of light. Therefore it is not surprising if his servants also disguise themselves as servants of righteousness, whose end will be according to their deeds" (cf. John 16:11).

Evidence in Our World

Indicators outside of Scripture also show the reality of Satan. First, Israel as a people, considering their relative insignificance in the history of the world, have been the continual, repeated victims of conquest and genocide, starting with the Persians (cf. Esther). The Greek conquest of Palestine was an attempt to destroy the Jewish culture with few parallels. From Haman through medieval pogroms to Hitler, Stalinization, and Islamic terrorism, these people have been a target. This conspiracy of hatred against the Jews is best explained as emanating from one sinister evil mind. This is to say nothing of the two millennia of attacks on Christian identity, purity, and community.

Second, the increase of demonic influence in our world requires an explanation. There is an increased unified conspiracy against God, His plan, and His people. This requires a personal unifying leader of a demonic force. Indeed, the Bible describes Satan as their "prince" (Luke 11:15) and "king" (Rev. 9:11). The increased evidence for true demonic possession further supports the reality of Satan and his demons.

Third, consider the universality of temptation and evil. Nothing else could account for heinous crimes committed by seemingly decent people. Law–abiding people, even some Christians, feel an urge to do horrendous evils totally out of keeping with their character. The universal temptation to sin, even by godly people, is best explained by a sustained, personal attack. A personification of evil or an impersonal force does not fit this picture. Magnetics is an impersonal force, but it does not personally allure.

Evil by its very nature interacts with intellect and will. Hence, the reality of a personal being such as Satan explains this.

Finally, through fallen angels (demons), there is a proliferation of deception in the world. The existence of thousands of false religions and cults testifies to the existence of a great Deceiver (1 Tim. 4:1–2).

Objections to Satan

Some object saying there are natural explanations for what is called "demonic" or evil. Often it is pointed out that what even the Bible called demonic is now known to have a natural cause.

However, this fails to understand that the Bible also distinguishes between natural sickness and demonic possession. Jesus differentiated between them when he listed them as separate miracles the Apostles were given power to do: "Heal the sick, raise the dead, cleanse the lepers, cast out demons" (Matt. 10:8). The Bible does not claim that all sickness is demonically caused. The Bible even recommends the use of medicine in treating natural sickness (cf. 1 Tim. 5:23). Similar symptoms may be present in sicknesses and some demon possessions, but that does not prove there is a natural explanation for both. The young man from whom a demon was cast in Matthew 17:14–17 had symptoms similar to those of an epileptic seizure, but that does not mean he had epilepsy. Similar effects do not prove identical causes. Both God and the magicians of Egypt turned water blood red. Even a demon–caused illness might respond to medicine. Many induced sicknesses can be treated. Because a mind caused it (whether human or demonic) does not mean medicine cannot relieve symptoms. At least some demonic activity manifests distinctive spiritual characteristics not present with natural sickness. These symptoms could include such things as opposition to God, violent reaction to Christ, and the manifestation of supernormal strength (cf. Mark 5:1–4). These do not respond to any purely natural treatment.

Others object saying that belief in Satan and demons is characteristic among the uneducated. These beliefs diminish as our society moves to a modern scientific understanding. However, this may partly be due to different strategies Satan uses among different peoples. He can adapt to the culture he is deceiving. What better way to deceive the sophisticated anti–supernaturalists than to lead them to believe he does not exist. The Bible declares that Satan disguises himself as an angel of light (2 Cor. 11:14). However, it is not true that demonic manifestations occur only among "primitive" people. With the "post–Christian age" the Western world has seen far more occult activity and reports of demonic manifestations.

His Names

Satan has many names in Scripture. He is the "Anointed cherub" (Eze. 28:14) who is perhaps the highest or class of angelic beings. He is the "Prince of this world" (John 12:31; 16:11) and therefore rules this world and opposes God's rule and kingdom. He is the "Prince and power of the air" (Eph. 2:2). Hence he is from above. He is the "god of this age" (2 Cor. 4:4) and his rule and influence is throughout time. He is "The Prince of Demons" (Matt. 12:24; Luke 11:15) and "Beelzebul" (means, "lord of the flies") which is an attempt to insult the gods of the Philistines. He is "Lucifer" (means, "shining one" Isa. 14:12). He is "Satan" (means "adversary" Zech. 3:1; Rev. 12:9) who is a self–proposed rival of the only true God; he is a counterfeit to the real. He is the "Devil" (means "slanderer" Luke 4:2; Rev. 12:9). He is one who trips up or defames God, Christ and believers. He is the "old serpent" (means "crafty") deceiver (2 Cor. 11:13–15) who leads minds astray (2 Cor. 11:30). He is the "Great dragon" (meaning "terrifying" Rev. 12:3, 7, 9) one who brings total devastation. He is the "Evil one" (John 17:15; 1 John 5:18) that clearly limits him to an individual person. He is the "Destroyer" (Rev. 9:11) of physical and spiritual life. A "Tempter" (Matt. 4:3; 1 Th. 3:5) who tries to entice men to evil. The "Accuser" (Job 1:9; Zech. 3:1; Rev. 12:10) who has access to God's presence and the "Deceiver" (Rev. 12:10, cf. Eph. 6:11) of the whole world.

His Personality

The nature of Satan is that of a created spirit (Col. 1:16) who is under judgment (John 12:31; Eph. 2:2). He is very powerful, but not omnipotent (see Table 2.1). He is very beautiful and uses this beauty to disguise his deception (2 Cor. 11:14). He is totally and permanently evil in a moral sense (John 17:50).

GOD	SATAN
Infinite	Finite
Uncreated	Created
All Good	Evil
All Knowing	Limited in Knowledge
All Present (everywhere)	Local Presence (here)
All Power	Limited Power
Create Life	Cannot Create Life
Miracles	Cannot do Miracles
Supernatural	Supernormal
Raise the Dead	Cannot Raise the Dead

Table 2.1

His Fall and Depravity

The depravity of Satan is pictured in the demise of the prince of Tyre. It begins with recognizing that he is originally created perfect (Ezek. 28:12, 13). He had a heavenly estate (Jude 6), the Garden of God or paradise. He was the guardian of God's glory (Ezek. 28:14; 2 Cor. 12:4). The occasion of his sin is his power and beauty. Ezekiel 28:16, 17 says, "By the abundance of your trade you were internally filled with violence, And you sinned; Therefore I have cast you as profane from the mountain of God. And I have destroyed you, O covering cherub, "Your heart was lifted up because of your beauty; you corrupted your wisdom by reason of your splendor. I cast you to the ground." The nature of his sin is pride. Isaiah 14:13–14 says, "I will make myself like the Most High." (cf. 1 Tim. 3:6). The cause of his sin is personal free choice. God cannot cause sin (Hab. 1:13; Jas 1:13), therefore there was no one else to temp him. The result was expulsion from heaven (Rev. 12:9; cf. Isa. 14:12), the corruption of his character (1 John 5:18; cf. Ezek. 28:15), perversion of his power (Eph. 2:2, cf. Isa. 14:12) which led to the defection of other angels (Rev. 12:4). This all leads to his final destruction (Rev. 20:10).

The time of Satan's sin is definitely before Adam (Gen. 3:1) and probably after the creation of the heavens (Gen. 1:10, cf. Job 38:7). Some have suggested it was on the second "day" of creation since this is the only day of which it is not said, "It was good."

In considering these things, we must not forget the overriding providence of God that reminds us that God created only good things (Gen. 3:1). Yet, God permitted evil and Satan (cf. Acts 17:30; 2 Peter 3:9) in order that He could produce a greater good. This is accomplished through Christ by defeating sin. Paul says in 1 Corinthians 15:25, "For He must reign until He has put all His enemies under His feet." Christ is able to destroy Satan. First John 3:8 says, "The one who practices sin is of the devil; for the devil has sinned from the beginning. The Son of God appeared for this purpose, to destroy the works of the devil." And Christ is able to redeem His servants. Paul says "but where sin increased, grace abounded all the more" (Rom. 5:20).

His Activity

Satan opposes God directly and indirectly. He directly opposes God by his original sin (Isa. 14) and slander (Job 1:9). He indirectly opposes God by attacking God's image in man (Gen. 3) and attacking God's word (Gen. 3:1). He attacks God's Son (Matt. 4:1) and God's program. Satan opposes God's program in heaven (Ezek. 28) and on earth. On earth he does this through false philosophies (Col. 2:8), false religions, specifically false "gospels" (Gal. 1:6, 8) and idolatry (1 Cor. 10:19, 20), false ministers (2 Cor. 11:14, 15), false doctrine (1 Tim. 4:1; 2 Peter 2:1), promoting schisms (2 Cor. 2:10, 11) and planting doubt (Gen. 3:1, 20).

Satan provokes us to sin through *pride*, 1 Timothy 3:6 says, "And not a new convert, so that he will not become conceited and fall into the condemnation incurred by the devil." We are provoked through *worry*, Matthew 13:22 says, "And the one on whom seed was sown among the thorns, this is the man who hears the word, and the worry of the world and the deceitfulness of wealth choke the word, and it becomes unfruitful." Through *self–reliance*, 1 Chronicles 21:1 says, "Now Satan stood up against Israel, and moved David to number Israel." Through *discouragement*, 1 Peter 5:6, 7 says "Therefore humble yourselves under the mighty hand of God, that He may exalt you at the proper time. Casting all your anxiety on Him, because He cares for you." Through *worldliness*, 1 John 2:16 says, "For all that is in the world, the lust of the flesh and the lust of the eyes and the boastful pride of life, is not from the Father, but is from the world" (cf. 5:19); and through *sexual sin*, 1 Corinthians 7:5 says "Stop depriving one another, except by agreement for a time, so that you may devote yourselves to prayer, and come together again so that Satan will not tempt you because of your lack of self-control."

Satanic Signs

The Bible uses the same words to describe Satan's power as those used for miracles (signs, wonders and power). However, Satan's powers are not divine. Indeed his signs are *counterfeit* wonders or miracles (2 Thess. 2:9). As we have seen, God's power is infinite but Satan's power is limited. Indeed, by the death and resurrection of Christ, Satan's power and authority has been disarmed and he has been destroyed (Col. 2:14; Heb. 2:14). However, Satan still works in the world awaiting his eternal sentence (Rev. 20).

Satan's power is not merely natural in the sense of mere physical forces. But neither are they supernatural in the sense that God is supernatural. Instead, the Bible calls them "spiritual forces" (Eph. 6:12) or "powers." Satan is the mastermind of evil. Just as humans can affect the physical world, so Satan's finite but super mind can do even more. However, he cannot do truly supernatural things as God can do. He cannot create life or raise the dead. He cannot suspend natural laws, but he can utilize them in unusual ways to achieve his evil purposes. From the book of Job, we know he can cause "fire . . . from the sky" and even "a mighty wind" (Job 1:12, 14, 19). Satan is the great counterfeiter and regularly tries to imitate what God can do. Satan cannot suspend natural laws (miracle), but he does try to convince people that he can. Satan is a master magician. He can perform tricks that should baffle the greatest magicians. He cannot do true miracles, but he can fool people into thinking he can. Indeed, what Satan does seems miraculous (Rev. 16:14). Jesus even pronounces doom on those who claimed: " 'Lord, Lord, did we not prophesy in Your name, and in Your name cast out demons, and in Your name perform many miracles?' " (Matt. 7:22).

We see how Satan's powers cannot equal God's in the contest between Moses and the Egyptian magicians. They could emulate only some of the signs but backed off when God by Moses' hand created life from dust (non-life). They confessed, "This is the finger of God" (Ex. 8:19). In short, the difference between a divine miracle and a satanic sign is as follows (Table 2.2).

DIVINE MIRACLE	SATANIC SIGN
Supernatural	Supernormal
Connected with truth	Connected with error
Associated with good	Associated with evil
Never associated with occult	Often associated with occult
Always successful	Not always successful

Table 2.2

Divine Miracle vs. Satanic Sign

How do we tell the difference between satanic signs and divine miracles? We must first make an important distinction between the truly supernatural and merely unusual. Every mystery is not a miracle. There are many things that are odd; but not everything that is odd is a miracle. Our world is filled with unusual and incredible occurrences. The vast majority of them have nothing to do with the supernatural or even the supernormal. The unexplained is not necessarily unexplainable. There are many kinds of unusual or odd events that have purely natural explanations.

Unusual events can be classified as anomalies, magic tricks, psychosomatic and even divine providence. An *anomaly* is something that has a natural cause in the world but is yet to be explained. The flight of the bumblebee once mystified scientists since its dimensions and wing size should have made flight impossible. *Magic* tricks involve the sleight of hand and fooling the eyes to appear to achieve the seemingly impossible. Professional magicians have even duplicated events considered by many to be paranormal. *Psychosomatic* is the effect of the mind on the body. Many illnesses and conditions are known to have purely psychological causes. *Providence* is God working through natural means or prearranged events to achieve His ends to give help to people. Many armies have benefited from having natural cover, fog for example, at just the right time on just the right day to achieve their victory. Indeed all of these are unusual. Hence, the unusual can be classified as follows (Table 2.3).

Much of what is called "supernatural" today is merely natural, explained or unexplained. However, we must not assume from this, however, that apart from true miracles all unusual events have purely physical causes. Simply because many unusual occurrences can be accounted for in this manner does not mean that all similar events can be so explained. We must guard against the fallacy of assuming that all such events have purely physical explanations.

	DESCRIPTION	POWER	EXAMPLE	TRAITS
Anomaly	Unexplained natural event	Nature	Flying bumblebee	Natural event, has a pattern
Magic	Deception, fooling	Human	Rabbit out of a hat	Human-controlled
Psychosomatic	Mind over matter	Mental	Psychosomatic cures	Requires faith, can fail, some sickness
Demonic	Evil power	Supernormal	Demonic influence	Evil, falsehood, occult, limited
Providential	Prearranged events	Divine	Fog in war to cover movement	Naturally explained, spiritual context
Miracle	Divine Act	Supernatural	Raising the dead	Never fails, immediate, lasts, brings glory to God

Table 2.3

There are spiritual beings, good and evil, that can cause highly unusual or supernormal events. Hence, we must be able to distinguish between the truly supernatural and the satanic supernormal.

A divine or biblical miracle is a truly supernatural act of God. It has God's fingerprints on it. These include:

A miracle is a supernatural act. True miracles transcend natural laws(s). They are a divine interference into the natural course of events. They are not simply unusual natural events. Instead, they are truly supernatural events. Miracles, such as those in the Bible, have the following characteristics:

- They were always immediate (Matt. 8:3).
- They were multiple, not just one (Acts 1:3)
- They were always successful with no relapses, even on incurable disease (John 4:46–54).
- They were connected with a truth claim in the name of God, confirming His nature or His word (Mark 2:10–11).
- They were often connected to a predicated element which always came to pass (John 13:19).

A miracle is always associated with truth. True miracles are never associated with false teaching. There is always a connection between the message and the miracles, between the sign and the sermon. Only in this way can they provide divine confirmation of a new revelation. The God of truth cannot confirm error. So false teaching is never connected with true miracles.

A miracle is always associated with good. Since God is moral goodness and miracles are His acts, it follows that miracles will manifest His moral character. It always brings glory to Him (John 2:11). If evil is manifested through a sign, then it is not a sign from God.

A miracle fits into nature. Miracles are supernatural but not *anti*natural. They are not square pegs in round holes; they always fit. They may speed up a natural process, but they never go against nature. For example, a miracle restores control or heals a human body by removing demons. God always uses them to further his purpose and design, such as showing Jesus is the Son of God.

In contrast to genuine miracles, we can see what a counterfeit sign is. A false sign differs from true miracles in the following ways.

A false sign is not supernatural. False signs are unusual. They may be supernormal, but they are not supernatural. As such,

- They are not always successful, they cannot cure the incurable.
- They are not immediate or instantaneous.
- There are relapses to the former conditions.
- A predicative element is not right.
- They are associated with error, evil or occult practices.

A false sign is associated with error. False signs and false teaching go together. Paul says, "But the Spirit explicitly says that in later times some will fall away from the faith, paying attention to deceitful spirits and doctrines of demons" (1 Tim. 4:1). There is a "spirit of truth and the spirit of error" (1 John 4:6). So a false teaching will never be confirmed by a true miracle. Only false signs will be connected with false teachings. Some of these include:

- Teaching that there are gods other than the one true God (Deut. 6:4; 13:1–3)
- Teaching the use of images or idols in worship (Ex. 20:3–4)
- Teaching that Jesus is not God (Col. 2:9)

- Teaching that Jesus did not come in human flesh (1 John 4:1–2)
- Teaching that we should contact departed spirits (Deut. 18:11)
- Teaching predications about the future that do not come to pass (Deut. 18:21–22)
- Teaching prophecy without Christ at the center (Rev. 19:10)

A false sign is associated with evil, immorality or occult practices. In Scripture, we find the following practices associated with false signs.

- Moral rebellion and anger with God (1 Sam. 15:23)
- Sexual immorality (Jude 7)
- Denying the use of sex within marriage (1 cor. 7:5; 1 Tim. 4:3)
- Legalism and self–denial (Col. 2:16–23)
- Lying (1 Tim. 4:2; John 8:44)
- Abstaining from certain foods on spiritual grounds (1 Tim. 4:3–4)
- Contacting departed spirits (Deut. 18:11)
- Use of channelers, mediums, or trances (Deut. 18:11; 1 Cor. 14:32)
- Encouraging self–deification (Gen. 3:5; 2 Thess. 2:9)
- Promoting astrology (Deut. 4:19; Isa. 47:13–15)

A false sign does not fit with nature. Indeed, they go against nature or are very odd. There is something *anti*-natural about them. They do not fit in the world. People, for example, should not have their bodies taken over by demons or have nature unusually take away their family, possessions and health, as it was with Job.

Not everything that is unusual is demonic and not everything that is unexplained is unexplainable. There are natural anomalies yet to be explained by science, human deception that involves hoaxing and trickery, and even divine providence, God working through natural means to achieve His ends. However, the unusual or supernormal connected with false teaching, error, evil or occult practices should, for sure, be considered Satanic in origin.

Summary

The study of Satan shows he is a spiritual creature that has freely rebelled against God and is therefore morally evil. He is active in our world promoting everything and anything opposed to the plan and goodness of God. He is providentially used by God to achieve His good ends. He is judged and defeated by the work of Christ on the cross. However, he can afflict and oppress believers and therefore, we must be able to distinguish his deceptive and false signs from true divine miracles and be on our guard equipped to engage in spiritual warfare.

Questions to Answer
1. What are some important biblical verses on the origin of Satan?
2. What are some important biblical verses on the nature of Satan?
3. What are some important biblical verses on the activity of Satan?
4. How do the abilities of Satan compare with God?
5. What makes a miracle different from a satanic sign?

3

Demons

You believe that God is one. You do well; the demons
also believe, and shudder.
James 2:1

Demons, like their chief leader Satan, are fallen angels with all their angelic powers (Chapter 1) pointed in opposition to God and His plan. This chapter investigates the origin, nature, and activity of demons. We conclude with a look at demon possession and spiritual warfare. Other questions about angels and demons are covered in the next chapter (4).

The Old Testament acknowledges the reality of demons. Deuteronomy 32:17 says, "They sacrificed to demons who were not God, . . ." Their activity as evil spirits is also acknowledged (1 Sam. 16:14–16). The New Testament mentions demons in every book, except Hebrews, and Christ affirmed their existence and gave authority to His disciples to cast them out (Matt. 10:1). Paul mentions that believers will judge them (1 Cor. 6:3). James says demons believe God is one and shudder (James 2:19).

THE ORIGIN AND FALL OF DEMONS

There are several false views concerning the origin of demons who are sometimes called unclean spirits (Matt. 17:18; Mark 9:25; Luke 10:17–20; Matt. 8:16). Some have supposed they are the spirits of deceased wicked people. This was an ancient Greek belief. However, both the Old and New Testament firmly assert that the deceased unsaved are confined in a place of torment. Psalm 9:17 says, "The wicked will return to Sheol, Even all the nations who forget God." Jesus teaches about the Rich man and Lazarus, in Luke 16:23 (cf. Rev. 20:13–14) saying, "In Hades he lifted up his eyes, being in torment, and saw Abraham far away and Lazarus in his bosom." Hence, nowhere in Scripture is their support for demons being the spirits of deceased wicked people.

Others have suggested that demons are the disembodied spirits of a pre–Adamic race. That is, they claim there was a race of humans before Adam. However, there is no biblical support for this assertion. Jesus taught in Matthew 19:4 saying, "Have you not read that He who created them from the beginning made them male and female." Hence, there is no possibility of humans existing before their creation as recorded in Genesis.

The final incorrect view is taken from Genesis 6:1–4. Some have argued that angels were the "sons of God" (which are angels in Job 1:6) married the daughters of men. The offspring of this unholy union, upon their judgment and death, became demons that exist today. However, there are other interpretations (see Chapter 4) such as the "sons of God" being humans or great ones on the earth. Even if it is a reference to angels, it is pointing to already fallen angels who possess human beings, who intermarry. Hence, it could not be the origin of demons.

The Correct View on the Origin of Demons

According to Scripture, demons are angels who rebelled with Satan. The book of Revelation says one third of all the angels fell with Satan (Rev. 12:4). There may even be two groups of rebellious demons. Those who are loose and active demons, Paul says,

> For our struggle is not against flesh and blood, but against the rulers, against the powers, against the world forces of this darkness, against the spiritual *forces* of wickedness in the heavenly *places*. (Eph. 6:11–12)

Satan is their prince (Matt. 12:24) and they even have a ranking that is similar to good angels (Eph. 3:10; 6:12). The second group of demons is confined. Indeed, some fear this confinement (Luke 8:31). For some demons it is permanent as is mentioned in 2 Peter 2:4: "For if God did not spare angels when they sinned, but cast them into hell and committed them to pits of darkness, reserved for judgment." Others may be only temporarily confined (Rev. 9:1–15).

THE NATURE OF DEMONS

The New Testament depicts demons with personal pronouns (Luke 8:27–30). They have an intellect, Paul says,

> But the Spirit explicitly says that in later times some will fall away from the faith, paying attention to deceitful spirits and doctrines of demons, by means of the hypocrisy of liars seared in their own conscience as with a branding iron, men who forbid marriage and advocate abstaining from foods which God has created to

be gratefully shared in by those who believe and know the truth. (1 Tim. 4:1–3),

Jesus' encounter with them as recorded in the Gospel of Luke shows they have a will,

> Now there was a herd of many swine feeding there on the mountain; and the demons implored Him to permit them to enter the swine. And He gave them permission. (Luke 8:32)

And emotions:

> Seeing Jesus, he cried out and fell before Him, and said in a loud voice, "What business do we have with each other, Jesus, Son of the Most High God? I beg You, do not torment me." (Luke 8:28)

Hence they have the full angelic capabilities but with a bent towards evil. They are further described as: "unclean spirits" (Matt. 10:1), "evil spirits" (Luke 7:21), "spirit of an unclean demon" (Luke 4:33), and "spiritual forces of wickedness" (Eph. 6:12). Although an appropriate description, they are never referred to in Scripture as "fallen angels."

As with all angels, bodies (flesh and blood) are not intrinsic to the nature of demons and their power is localized. They can appear or make their presence known by various means (Acts 19:15; Rev. 9:1–12; 16:13). However, the lack of appearance of demons materially may suggest that they are unable or prevented from doing so. Demons seem to seek embodiment in physical beings through possession (Matt. 8:28–32) and this may be because of their inability to materialize.

THE ACTIVITIES OF DEMONS

The powers of demons include super–human or super-normal displays especially in possessed humans. The Gospel of Mark records such an encounter,

> When He got out of the boat, immediately a man from the tombs with an unclean spirit met Him, and he had his dwelling among the tombs. And no one was able to bind him anymore, even with a chain; because he had often been bound with shackles and chains, and the chains had been torn apart by him and the shackles broken in pieces, and no one was strong enough to subdue him. (Mark 5:3; cf. Acts 19:16).

Their intellect can pretend to predict the future (Acts 16:16). They can enter or possess human and animal bodies (Luke 8:30). They are limited, not infinite, even in their collective influence. They have supernormal power to do false signs and wonders. Paul says of the antichrist, "That is, the one whose coming is in accord with the activity of Satan, with all power and signs and false wonders" (2 Thess. 2:9).

The overall goal of demons is to follow Satan in promoting everything and anything opposed to the plan and goodness of God. This is achieved through specific activities identified in Scripture. They extend Satan's activities (Eph. 6:11–12), oppose the plan of God (Dan. 10:10–14; Rev. 16:13–16) and promote idolatry (Lev. 17:7; Deut. 32:17; 1 Cor. 10:20). They instigate false religions, teach against the incarnation and resurrection. John says,

> By this you know the Spirit of God: every spirit that confesses that Jesus Christ has come in the flesh is from God; and every spirit that does not confess Jesus is not from God. (1 John 4:1–4)

Paul says,

> the Spirit explicitly says that in later times some
> will fall away from the faith, paying attention
> to deceitful spirits and doctrines of demons, by
> means of the hypocrisy of liars seared in their
> own conscience as with a branding iron, men
> who forbid marriage and advocate abstaining
> from foods which God has created to be
> gratefully shared in by those who believe and
> know the truth. (1 Tim. 4:1–3)

Hence, demons are even against salvation by faith alone since some fall away from the faith by "paying attention to deceitful spirits and doctrines of demons." They are against what is morally right and promote acts of immorality (Rev. 2:20–24). They are also used by God (Judg. 9:23; 1 Sam. 16:14; 1 Kings 22:22; 2 Cor. 12:7) to achieve His good ends.

In relation to people in general they can cause affliction through physical disease (Matt. 9:33; 12:22; 17:15–18), mental disorder (Mark 5:4–5; 9:22; Luke 8:27–29; 9:37–42) and death (Rev. 9:14–19). However, it is important to note that not all illness is demonic (Matt. 4:24; Mark 1:32; Luke 7:21; 9:1). They can cause perversion through promoting immoral life styles (1 Tim. 4:1–3), through individual evil activities (Deut. 32:17; Ps. 106:37–39) and even through the nations (Lev. 18:6–30; Deut. 18:9–14).

Activities in Relation to Believers

In relation to believers and the church they can tempt us to sin and rely on our flesh. James describes the process:

> Let no one say when he is tempted, "I am being
> tempted by God"; for God cannot be tempted
> by evil, and He Himself does not tempt anyone.

> But each one is tempted when he is carried away
> and enticed by his own lust. Then when lust has
> conceived, it gives birth to sin; and when sin
> is accomplished, it brings forth death. (James
> 1:13–15)

And he gives the solution:

> Submit therefore to God. Resist the devil and
> he will flee from you. Draw near to God and He
> will draw near to you. Cleanse your hands, you
> sinners; and purify your hearts, you double-
> minded. (James 4:7–8)

The Apostle John says, "For all that is in the world, the lust of the flesh and the lust of the eyes and the boastful pride of life, is not from the Father, but is from the world" (1 John 2:16).

Paul explains,

> For this is the will of God, your sanctification;
> that is, that you abstain from sexual immorality;
> that each of you know how to possess his own
> vessel in sanctification and honor, not in lustful
> passion, like the Gentiles who do not know God.
> (1 Thess. 4:3–5; cf. 1 Cor. 5:1–5; Eph. 2:2–3; 1
> Tim. 3:6)

Paul attributes some inflicted maladies to Satan (e.g., Paul's "thorn in the flesh" – 2 Cor. 12:7–9; cf. Job 2:7–9) and the hindrance of ministry travel (1 Thess. 2:18). Satan and demons create division (Eph. 4:3) including doctrinal division (1 John 4:1–4; 1 Tim. 4:3–4, 8; 2 Tim. 3:5; 2 Peter 2:1–2). They promote jealousy and selfish ambitions (1 Cor. 3:1–4). Paul says, "If I have forgiven anything, I did it for your sakes in the presence of Christ, so that no advantage would be taken of us by Satan, for we are not ignorant of his schemes" (2 Cor. 2:10). Demons counter and pervert the gospel. Paul says,

> And even if our gospel is veiled, it is veiled to
> those who are perishing, in whose case the
> god of this world has blinded the minds of the
> unbelieving so that they might not see the light
> of the gospel of the glory of Christ, who is the
> image of God. (2 Cor. 4:3–4; cf. vv. 14–15)

Satan and demons can even be the cause of persecution (Rev. 2:8–10).

DEMON POSSESSION

Demonic possession or demonized is when a demon, or more than one, is exercising their will or power, in control of a human being. The Gospels contain numerous instances of demonic possession. A major part of Jesus' earthly ministry was devoted to casting out demons. Matthew records, "When evening came, they brought to Him many who were demon-possessed; and He cast out the spirits with a word, and healed all who were ill" (Matt. 8:16; cf. Matt. 8:28; 9:32; 12:22; 15:22; Mark 1:32; 5:15; Luke 8:36). The Apostles ministry also involved casting out demons (Acts 16:16; 19:13). Demons can produce muteness, blindness, and convulsions (Matt. 9:32; 12:22; Luke 9:36), tendencies to self–destruction (Mark 5:5; Luke 9:42), insanity (John 10:20), supernormal strength (Mark 5:3–4), and occult power (Acts 16:16–18).

A scriptural distinction is made when an illness is demonic as opposed to a natural illness that is a cause of physical disease, mental disorders and death. Acts 5:16 says, "the people from the cities in the vicinity of Jerusalem were coming together, bringing people who were *sick and afflicted with unclean spirits*, and they were all being healed" (emphasis added).

Demonic possession of a believer does not seem well supported in Scripture. No believer, who is indwelt by the Spirit of God (1 Cor. 6:19 cf. 2 Cor. 6:14–18), can have a demon at the same time. This is especially true given what is done on the behalf of the believer by the Holy Spirit at the moment of salvation. The believer becomes the *possession* of God through sealing (2 Cor. 1:22; Eph. 1:13–14) and the permanent indwelling (John 14:16) of the third person of the Trinity. The believer has the present and permanent possession of eternal life (John 5:24). John says, "We know that no one who is born of God sins; but He who was born of God keeps him, and the evil one does not touch him" (1 John 5:18). Paul says, "For He [Christ] rescued us from the domain [or authority] of darkness, and transferred us to the kingdom of His beloved Son" (Col. 1:13). Given this, demonic possession seems limited to unbelievers

However, demonic oppression, attack from without, is a possible reality for a believer and can be quite sever (Job 1:11; 2:5, 9; Luke 22:31–32). Believers may experience *oppression* or be influenced by demons, but there is no clear example of a believer being possessed or demonized. Possession is the direct willful control of a person's body by a demon. In oppression, demons attack from the outside, not the inside.

Some object saying that when Jesus spoke to Peter and said, "Get behind Me, Satan! You are a stumbling block to Me; for you are not setting your mind on God's interests, but man's" (Matt. 16:23) that Peter was possessed by Satan. However, it is more likely Jesus is seeing Peter's words as reminiscent of Satan's previous temptation to circumvent the cross (Matt. 4:8-10). Satan certainly is influencing this, but without possession. Others say that Ananias, a believer was possessed because Peter said, "Ananias, why has Satan filled your heart to lie to the Holy Spirit and to keep back some of the price of the land?" (Acts 5:3). However, the term "filled" can mean *influenced* as it does elsewhere in Acts and the Gospels. (cf. Acts 2:28; John 11:16).

There are no instances where the clear terminology of possession such as "demonized," "to have" a demon, or "cast out" are ever used in connection with someone who is clearly a believer. Indeed, it says of Judas "Satan then entered into him" (John 13:27), but there is good reason to hold Judas was not a believer (John 17:12; Acts 1:16; Ps. 41:9).

Spiritual Warfare

Some Scripture seems to suggest that God is the cause of evil spirits or demons (1 Sam. 16:15) and may even use occult divination (1 Sam. 28:7f) as in the story of Saul who consulted the medium of Endor. However, God is the ultimate efficient causation of all things and God uses even evil (as secondary causes) for achieving His good ends. Saul was rebuked for what he did and the occult means is consistently condemned in Scripture.

Consider the following explicit prohibitions that involve the demonic:

- Denying the word of God, the Serpent (Satan) questioned, "Indeed, has God said, . . . ?" (Gen. 3:1)
- Denying death, Satan said, "You surely will not die" (Gen. 3:4).
- Encouraging self–deification,

    For God knows that in the day you eat from it your eyes will be opened, and you will be like God, knowing good and evil. (Gen. 3:5; cf. 2 Thess. 2:9)

- Advocating astrology,

  > And beware not to lift up your eyes to heaven and
  > see the sun and the moon and the stars, all the
  > host of heaven, and be drawn away and worship
  > them and serve them, those which the Lord your
  > God has allotted to all the peoples under the
  > whole heaven. (Deut. 4:19; cf. Isa. 47:13–15).

- Making false predictions,

  > When a prophet speaks in the name of the Lord,
  > if the thing does not come about or come true,
  > that is the thing which the Lord has not spoken.
  > The prophet has spoken it presumptuously; you
  > shall not be afraid of him. (Deut. 18:21–22)

- Contacting departed spirits and using instruments
  of divination,

  > There shall not be found among you anyone who
  > makes his son or his daughter pass through the
  > fire, one who uses divination, one who practices
  > witchcraft, or one who interprets omens, or a
  > sorcerer, or one who casts a spell, or a medium,
  > or a spiritist, or one who calls up the dead. For
  > whoever does these things is detestable to the
  > Lord; and because of these detestable things the
  > Lord your God will drive them out before you.
  > (Deut. 18:10–12)

- Advocating idolatry of images,

  > You shall have no other gods before Me. You shall
  > not make for yourself an idol, or any likeness of
  > what is in heaven above or on the earth beneath
  > or in the water under the earth. (Ex. 20:3–4;)

  > If a prophet or a dreamer of dreams arises among
  > you and gives you a sign or a wonder, and the
  > sign or the wonder comes true, concerning
  > which he spoke to you, saying, 'Let us go after
  > other gods (whom you have not known) and let
  > us serve them, you shall not listen to the words of
  > that prophet or that dreamer of dreams; for the
  > Lord your God is testing you to find out if you

love the Lord your God with all your heart and
with all your soul. (Deut. 13:1–3)

- Denial of Christ's humanity or deity, "For in Him
  [Jesus Christ] all the fullness of Deity dwells in
  bodily form." (Col. 2:9)

  > By this you know the Spirit of God: every spirit
  > that confesses that Jesus Christ has come in the
  > flesh is from God; and every spirit that does
  > not confess Jesus is not from God; this is the
  > spirit of the antichrist. (1 John 4:1–2)

- Depreciating or denying marriage and advocating
  abstinence from certain foods for religious reasons,

  > Men who forbid marriage and advocate
  > abstaining from foods which God has created
  > to be gratefully shared in by those who believe
  > and know the truth. For everything created by
  > God is good, and nothing is to be rejected if it is
  > received with gratitude. (1 Tim. 4:3–4)

- Promoting immorality,

  > In which you formerly walked according to the
  > course of this world, according to the prince of
  > the power of the air, of the spirit that is now
  > working in the sons of disobedience. Among
  > them we too all formerly lived in the lusts of
  > our flesh, indulging the desires of the flesh and
  > of the mind, and were by nature children of
  > wrath, even as the rest. (Eph. 2:2–3; cf. Jude 7)

- Encouraging legalistic self–denial,

  > Let no one keep defrauding you of your prize by
  > delighting in self–abasement and the worship
  > of the angels, taking his stand on visions he
  > has seen, inflated without cause by his fleshly
  > mind, . . . (Col. 2:18; cf. 2:16–23)

- Promoting lying,

> You are of your father the devil, and you want to do the desires of your father. He was a murderer from the beginning, and does not stand in the truth because there is no truth in him. Whenever he speaks a lie, he speaks from his own nature, for he is a liar and the father of lies. (John 8:44)

John describes the method of Satan's attacks:

> Do not love the world nor the things in the world. If anyone loves the world, the love of the Father is not in him. For all that is in the world, the lust of the flesh and the lust of the eyes and the boastful pride of life, is not from the Father, but is from the world. The world is passing away, and also its lusts; but the one who does the will of God lives forever. (1 John 2:15–17)

They do not usually come as a direct attack from Satan or demons; instead, the attack usually come indirectly from the world and through the lust of our flesh (Figure 3.1).

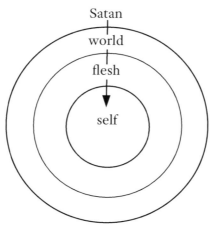

Figure 3.1

Ephesians 6:10–20, provides a reminder of the weapons that Christian's must daily use to combat spiritual warfare. The warfare is not physical, but just as real. The spiritual enemy is the devil, his schemes, spiritual forces of the world and wickedness. The believer's protection and fight, begins by living in the Spirit (Eph. 4–6). Paul says,

> You lay aside the old self, which is being corrupted in accordance with the lusts of deceit, and that you be renewed in the spirit of your mind, and put on the new self, which in the likeness of God has been created in righteousness and holiness of the truth. (Eph. 4:22–24)

Paul then uses a description of the armor found on a Roman soldier to stress the importance of our spiritual armor. As any soldier knows, in war, he must stand firm and this involves putting on their whole armor. Likewise, Paul says Christians must put on the whole armor of God that includes:

1. The Breastplate of righteousness – which is likely a reference to living in light of our righteous standing or position in Christ, since we are righteous before God only because of the substitutionary work of Christ on the cross.

2. The Belt of Truth – holds the armor together and provides readiness to answer Satan's lies with truth, hence we must know the truth of Scripture.

3. The Sandals – are the soldier's feet, which likely concern our readiness and willingness to share the peace of God through evangelism as we go or move.

4. The Shield of Faith – is the large defensive weapon used to hold a Roman soldier's composure and enables him to make a military advance. As the enemy, Satan and his demons, are sure to aim at us, our faith, trust in God, must be used to hold our composure and make spiritual advances even while under attack.

5. The Helmet of Salvation – is the protective helmet of a soldier. Our attitude must be one of thoughtful dependence on the salvation of God, that He has provided which will be manifest upon His return in glory.

6. The Sword of the Spirit – a sword is the basic weapon of the Roman soldier. For us it is the word of God (the whole Bible). It refers to saying and believing God's word to counter Satan (as Christ did Matt. 4:1–11).

7. Prayer – is the means of communication with our Lord. We make requests, show dependence and recognize that prayer is the only means of bringing defeat on the enemy (Satan).

Persevering in these will protect us from the evil one and his daily attacks. The Devil is defeated and if we submit ourselves to God and resist him, he will flee from us (James 4:7).

SUMMARY

The study of demons shows they are numerous spiritual creatures that have freely rebelled against God and are therefore morally evil. They are active in our world, like Satan, promoting everything and anything opposed to the plan and goodness of God. They are providentially used by God to achieve His good ends. They have been judged and defeated by the work of Christ on the cross. However, they can afflict and oppress believers and therefore, we must be on our guard equipped to engage in spiritual warfare.

Questions to Answer
1. What biblical verses support the origin of demons?
2. What biblical verses support the nature and activity of demons?
3. What is the difference between demon *oppression* and demon *possession*?
4. What can demons do and not do to believers?
5. What must believers do to fight spiritual warfare?

4

Questions and Answers
on Angels, Satan & Demons

*Let love of the brethren continue. Do not neglect to show
hospitality to strangers, for by this some have enter-
tained angels without knowing it. Remember the prison-
ers, as though in prison with them, and those who are
ill–treated, since you yourselves also are in the body.*
Hebrews 13:1–3

In this chapter, we provide brief answers to some of the
most popular questions asked about angels, Satan and
demons.

QUESTIONS ABOUT ANGELS

Can we prove that angels exist?

We cannot prove the existence of angels the same way
we can prove the existence of God apart from the Bible
by using philosophical arguments. Some philosophers
tried to demonstrate that angels must exist by arguing for
a great chain of being and that God must (being perfect)
create the best possible world of creatures which includes

angels. However, it seems better to reason **not** that they *must* exist but that they *do* exist. God is perfectly free to create anything that is possible. By divine revelation, the Bible, we know that angels do exist. Therefore, angels exist. Hence, this argument rests on the Bible being the word of God. Another way to show the existence of angels is based on the teaching of Jesus Christ. What Jesus Christ (Son of God) teaches is true. Jesus Christ teaches the existence of angels.

> Jesus answered and said to them [Sadducees], "You are mistaken, not understanding the Scriptures nor the power of God. For in the resurrection they neither marry nor are given in marriage, but are like angels in heaven. (Matt. 22:29–30)

Hence, Jesus taught the truth of the resurrection and existence of angels against the Sadducees who denied both. Therefore, angels exist.

Do angels have spiritual bodies (1 Cor. 15:44) and wings?

Angels are created simple spirts that do not have bodies or matter that is essential to their nature. They are intellects or minds without bodies. They do not have any qualities or characteristics that are not essential to their nature such as size, shape, age, color, etc. They are not subject to decay and death, since they have no material body. They do not learn and grow at least the way humans can. Paul uses the term "spiritual body" to emphasize the dominance of a resurrected physical body being supernaturally controlled. He uses the same term to describe a "spiritual rock" (1 Cor. 10:4). Paul is not saying there is such a thing as an immaterial body. He is saying the resurrection body is dominated or controlled by the spirit. It is interesting that not all angels are depicted in Scripture with wings (Dan. 9:21; Rev. 14:6). Such depictions in Scripture may involve materialization, visualization, bodily assumption, or be a symbol for their swiftness.

Can angels die?

Angels are simple beings with no bodies or parts. If death is understood as the separation of the soul from the body, then angels cannot die since they have no material bodies. They are immortal by nature. They have a beginning, but no end (or are aeviternal). Hence, they cannot die (i.e., separation of spirit/body). The only change they can undergo is being brought into existence by God or caused to go out of existence by God. However, the Bible is clear that angels, like humans, will not be annihilated. Luke 20:36 says, "They can no longer die; for they are like the angels . . ." Evil angels, like unbelievers, will be judged and kept in conscious confinement (hell) for all eternity (Matt. 25:41).

Can angels do miracles?

God can do miracles through angels (Gen. 19:11), just as he did through human Apostles and prophets (Heb. 2:4). But only God can do the supernatural. Angels have greater power than humans, which can be called supernormal. However, just as humans, they cannot do the truly supernatural unless God is doing it through them. Indeed, even the Egyptian magicians were unable to do what only the "finger of God" could do, when it came to the plagues that created life from non-life (Ex. 8:19).

Will we be angels in heaven?

Human death is the separation of the soul from the body. Jesus said in such a state we are "like" the angels in heaven (Matt. 22:30). Paul said, to be absent from the body, is to be home with the Lord (2 Cor. 5:8). However, this is only a temporary state until the resurrection (1 Thess. 4:16). A human being is the union of soul and body. So, in the resurrection, our soul will be united to the same material body we had on earth, although glorified (1 Cor. 15). Paul says that in our glorified state we will rule with and judge angels: "Do you not know that we will judge angels? How much more matters of this life?" (1 Cor. 6:2–3).

How is one angel different from another angel?

Each angel is a finite simple (non-complex) created being. They cannot reproduce after their kind (Matt. 22:30). They have no body, size, shape, etc. Therefore, the only way they can differ is in the amount and comprehensiveness of their knowledge, which God gives them. This makes each individual angel its own species or kind, thus giving reason for their rank as lower and higher, inferior and superior, based on their intellect or knowledge.

Do angels minister to believers?

Yes. Scripture affirms that angels do many things for believers. Some of these include:

1. Communicate God's word (Acts 7:52–53; Gal. 3:19).

2. Meet physical needs (Gen 21:17–20; Ps 78:23–25).

3. Provide protection and deliverance (Gen 32:1–32; Rev 7:1–14).

4. Provide strength and encouragement (Acts 5:19–20).

5. Watch over children (Matt. 18:10).

6. Promote evangelism (Acts 8:26).

7. Restrain wickedness (Gen. 18:22).

8. Announce and execute judgment (Rev. 8, 14, 16, 19).

9. Involved in answering prayer (Acts 12:7).

10. Care for believers at death (Luke 16:22).

Does the Bible teach (1 Thess. 4:16) that Jesus is Michael the archangel?

Despite strong reason given in the book of Hebrews (1–2) that Jesus is superior to all angels and not of the same nature (see Chapter 1), some, especially Jehovah's Witnesses, teach that Jesus is Michael the archangel. They say Jesus makes the command for the resurrection being described as "with the voice of the archangel" (1 Thess. 4:16) and Jude 9 says the archangel is Michael. However, a careful look at the verse shows Jesus does not speak but that He descends from heaven when the voice of the archangel speaks. The archangel Michael will accompany Jesus' coming at the rapture; since it is the archangel's voice (not Jesus') that issues the shout (2 Thess. 1:7). Jesus created the archangel Michael, just as He did all other angels (Col 1:16), so he and the other angels worship Jesus (Heb. 1:6).

Is Satan, being evil, just as powerful as God?

No! God created Satan (Col. 1:16). Satan is a finite spirit and morally evil. He is limited in knowledge and power. Satan is powerful, but only God is all–powerful, infinite, uncreated, all good, all knowing and present everywhere. Only God can create life, do miracles or the supernatural. Satan only has a local presence and limited power. Satan cannot create life. He can do the supernormal according to his limited spiritual power, but he cannot do the truly supernatural (miraculous).

GOD	SATAN
Infinite	Finite
Uncreated	Created
All Good	Evil
All Knowing	Limited in Knowledge
All Present (everywhere)	Local Presence (here)
All Power	Limited Power
Create Life	Cannot Create Life
Miracles	Cannot do Miracles
Supernatural	Supernormal
Raise the Dead	Cannot Raise the Dead

How could a perfect creature made by a perfect God in a perfect environment (heaven) commit a sin?

Sin arose from Satan's free will. God made perfect creatures and gave them perfect natures and perfect freedom. But with freedom, though good in itself, comes the ability to sin. Therefore, sin arose from the free will of Satan in the presence of God. Freedom is good, but it contains the possibility of evil. God made a perfectly good angel, and the perfectly good angel made evil. God gave the *fact* of freedom (which is good); Satan performed the *act* of freedom to rebel against God (which is evil).

Can Satan know what is in my heart (mind)?

No. One of the clear indicators of the divine nature is the ability to know what is in the heart of men (Heb. 4:13-12). The Old Testament acknowledged this,

> Whatever prayer or supplication is made by any man or by all Your people Israel, each knowing the affliction of his own heart, and spreading his hands toward this house; then hear in heaven Your dwelling place, and forgive and act and render to each according to all his ways, whose heart You know, for You [God] *alone* know the hearts of all the sons of men. (1 Kings 8:38–39, emphasis added)

The New Testament uses this as an indicator of the divine nature of Jesus Christ. John says,

> But Jesus, on His part, was not entrusting Himself to them, for He knew all men, and because He did not need anyone to testify concerning man, for He Himself knew what was in man. (John 2:24–25)

Hence, only the Triune God can know what is in any human heart. Satan and demons while certainly intelligent and powerful, scheming and deceitful, do not know what is in a person's heart (mind).

Does divination or predicting the future with demons work?

Divination is the practice of foretelling future events or discovering hidden knowledge by occult means. This is usually attempted by astrology, palmistry, card playing, visions, Ouija boards, crystal balls, and an assortment of magic objects. Scripture warns against divination and all other occult activity (Deut. 18:9–14). Divination has its source in the demonic. Acts 16 records an account of a slave girl who had a "spirit of divination." However, her ability for fortune–telling ceased after Paul cast a demon out of her in the name of Jesus (Acts 16:18). God is the only one who can reveal or predict the future with 100% accuracy. That is, give prophecy that never fails. God alone is sovereign over time and space. Indeed, Isaiah says,

> I, the Lord, am the maker of all things, stretching out the heavens by Myself and spreading out the earth all alone, causing the omens of boasters to fail, making fools out of diviners, causing wise men to draw back and turning their knowledge into foolishness. (Isaiah 44:24–25)

Christians must not come under the grip of Satan, through any occult involvement. All comfort and security should come from God alone (Lev. 19:31).

How can Satan and God both be the cause of something?

The Bible for example, seems at times to credit both God and Satan, as being the cause of David's numbering the people of Israel and Judah (2 Sam. 24:1; 1 Chron. 21:1). This is explained by seeing that Satan was the immediately influence on David, but ultimately God permitted Satan to carry out the provocation. Satan desired to destroy David and the people of God. However, God used this to humble David and the people to teach them a valuable spiritual lesson. Similar descriptions are made of Job in which God and Satan are involved in his sufferings (Job 1–2). Indeed, God and Satan are involved in the crucifixion of Jesus. Satan's purpose is to destroy the Son of

God (John 13:2). God's purpose is to redeem humankind by the death of His Son (Acts 2:14–39).

How can Satan come before God's throne if he was thrown out of heaven?

The book of Job (1:6) seems to imply that Satan has access to the throne of God but elsewhere in Scripture, he was banished from God's presence (Rev. 12:7–12). Satan was *officially* expelled from heaven, but he still *actually* has access there. Scripture presents the idea that Satan has access to the presence of God to accuse believers (Zach. 3:1). Revelation 12:10 shows Satan as the accuser of the brethren. Satan appears before God to accuse God's people of sin. This is what he was doing against Job (Job 1:6; 2:1). Ultimately, Satan will be cast into the lake of fire forever (Rev. 20:10).

Does Satan have the power of death or does God?

Hebrews 2:14 says, "That through death He might render powerless him who had the power of death, that is, the devil." In other places it says that only God has the power over life and death (Deut. 32:39; cf. Job 1:21). God is sovereign over all life. Only God can create life and only He has determined the number of our days (Ps. 90:10–12) and appointed the day of our death (Heb. 9:27). However, Satan by tempting Adam and Even succeeded in bring on God's pronounced judgment of death on humanity. (Gen. 2:17; Rom. 5:12). Therefore, Satan, in a sense, can be said to have had the power of death (Heb. 2:14). But indeed, it is Christ who now holds "the keys of Hades and Death" (Rev. 1:18) since he has tasted death for every man (Heb. 2:9) and rose triumphantly from the grave (Rom. 4:25).

QUESTIONS ABOUT DEMONS

Why can't angels who sinned and became demons be saved?

Salvation was offered to Adam after he sinned (Gen. 3:15), why some wonder, was it not offered to Satan and his following demons. The biblical answer as to the salvation of angels is a clear *no* for the following reasons: First, the Bible emphatically says, "For assuredly He does not give help to angels, but He gives help to the descendant of Abraham." (Heb. 2:16). Christ assumed human nature (Heb. 2:14) not an angelic nature, to redeem human beings, not angels. Second, Paul says that the cross of Christ, which is the source of human salvation, is by contrast the source of condemnation for demons. He writes,

> Having canceled out the certificate of debt consisting of decrees against us, which was hostile to us; and He has taken it out of the way, having nailed it to the cross. When He had disarmed the rulers and authorities, He made a public display of them, having triumphed over them through Him. (Col. 2:14–15)

Third, the lost state of demons is consistently portrayed in the Bible as final and eternal. Peter says, "For if God did not spare angels when they sinned, but cast them into hell and committed them to pits of darkness, reserved for judgment" (2 Peter 2:4; cf. Jude 6; Matt. 8:29; Rev. 12:12).

Finally, theologians argue that since angels are unchangeable in their nature and knowledge, there is no way for them to be redeemed; such would require a change of mind. Once they make up their minds, it is fixed forever, just as ours is at death (Heb. 9:27).

Is it unfair that God did not offer salvation to demons?

Similar to human beings, angels have a choice in their destiny. They freely chose to rebel against God; they were not forced to do so against their will. Also, like humans angels were only doomed after their final choice. The difference is that the first choice of angels was also their final choice. Humans also have a cutoff point (Heb. 9:27). Angels, as we have shown (Chapter 1) are created as simple beings. Therefore, once angels make a choice to serve or rebel against God, it is permanent, just as it is permanent for humans (by death). Angels are never called to repent, as human beings are (Acts 17:30). In short, what is a lifetime for us is an instant for an angel. Once their free choice is made up, it is permanent; since they cannot change. God knowing this had no need to provide salvation for them.

Where the "sons of God" in Genesis 6 angels (demons) who married women?

The phrase "sons of God" (Gen. 6:2) seems to refer to angels (Job 1:6; 2:1; 38:7). The Greek Old Testament (LXX) translates this "angels" and the New Testament may be referring to these as angels (2 Peter 2:4; Jude 6–7). Yet, the New Testament says angels "neither marry nor are given in marriage" (Matt. 22:30). There are several interpretations that do not insist that angels cohabitated with women. Some scholars see "sons of God" as referring to the godly line of Seth (from whom the redeemer would come – Gen. 4:26). This line intermingled with the godless line of Cain. Humans are referred to in the Bible as God's "sons" (Isa. 43:6; Luke 3:38; Gal. 3:26). This seems to fit the immediate context and it avoids the problem with seeing them as angels. Other scholars see

"sons of God" as referring to great men of old, men of re-
nown. The text refers to "giants" and "mighty men" (Gen.
6:4). This also avoids the problem of angels cohabitation
with humans. Some scholars even combine these views
and speculate that the "sons of God" were angels who
possessed human beings that interbreed with "the daughters of men" thus producing the "giants" and "men of re-
nown." This view seems to explain all the data and avoids
the problem that angels as such bodiless (Heb. 1:14) and
sexless spirits (Matt. 22:30) cohabited with women.

Who were the "spirits in prison" that Jesus preached to after His death in 1 Peter 3:19?

First Peter 3:19 says, Christ, after His death on the
cross, "went and made proclamation to the spirits now
in prison." Regardless of who *they* ("spirits . . . in prison") are, we should observe that the passage does not say
Christ *evangelized* them, but simply that he *proclaimed*
the victory of His resurrection to them. This is not an
instance of evangelism after death, which is not taught
in the Bible (Heb. 9:27; 2 Cor. 6:2). Some do take the
phrase "spirits in prison" to refer to fallen angels where
Peter mentions angels sinning (2 Peter 2:4–5) in the time
of Noah. They point out that nowhere else is this phrase
used of human beings in hell. Others, however, teach that
Christ preached through the person of Noah to those
who, because they rejected his message, are now spirits
in prison (cf. 1 Peter 1:11; 2 Peter 2:5). Hence, this view
sees the Spirit of Christ preaching through Noah to the
ungodly people who now await final judgment. However,
another interpretation is that this is referring to Christ's
announcement to departed spirits (humans) of the tri-
umph of His resurrection, declaring to them the victory
He achieved by His death and resurrection. This seems

to fit the context (1 Peter 3:18), accords with the rest of Scripture (cf. Eph. 4:8; Col. 2:15) and avoids problems with the other views.

Are demons bound or free to tempt humans?

Peter speaks of demons that are confined and reserved for judgment (2 Peter 2:4) yet other places in the New Testament speaks of demons who roam free over the earth oppressing and even possessing people (Matt. 12:22; 17:14–17; Acts 16:16–18; Rev. 16:14). There are at least two ways to explain this. First, Peter may be speaking of the official and ultimate end of demons as opposed to their actual and immediate status. That is, even though God sentenced them to eternal damnation, they are not yet serving their term (Matt. 8:29). Second, another possibility is that Peter may be speaking of a different class of fallen angels already confined as opposed to the rest of the demons that are loose.

Can demons perform miracles?

Revelation 16:14 says, "For they are spirits of demons, performing signs, which go out to the kings of the whole world." The Bible sometimes uses the same words (signs, wonders, power) as those used to describe miracles of God (2 Thess. 2:9). However, a miracle is a supernatural act of God, and only God can do miracles. Demons are created beings with limited power. Demons and Satan have great spiritual powers, but there is a gigantic difference between their power and the power of God. God is infinite power, the devil and demons are finite and limited. Only God can create life (Gen. 1:1, 21; Deut. 32:39). Satan and demons cannot (Ex. 8:19). Only God can raise the dead (John 10:18; Rev. 1:18). Satan and demons cannot. The best Satan can do is give animation "breath" to the idolatrous image of the Antichrist (Rev. 13:15). Satan and demons can do the *supernormal* but not the *supernatural*. The spiritual power of Satan and demons is given to them by God and is carefully limited and monitored (Job 1:10–12). Since Christ has defeated Satan and triumphed over him and all his demons (Heb. 2:14–15; Col. 2:15), Jesus Christ gives power to His people to be victorious over demonic forces (Eph. 4:4–11). Indeed, as John says, "You are from God, little children, and have overcome them; because greater is He [God] who is in you than he [Satan] who is in the world" (1 John 4:4).

Does demon possession occur today?

Yes, Scripture nowhere indicates that demonic possession has ceased, indeed, it says that in the last days, there will be an abundance of demonic activity. Paul says "But the Spirit explicitly says that in later times some will fall away from the faith, paying attention to deceitful spirits and doctrines of demons" (1 Tim. 4:1; cf. 2 Peter 2:1; Jude 4). However, not everyone who thinks they are possessed by a demon really is. Many could be influenced by drugs, hallucinating, or have other natural or psychological problems. Even Scripture distinguishes between a natural illness and the demonic (Matt. 4:24; Mark 1:32; Luke 7:21; 9:1). However, some cases cannot be totally explained in normal ways. Even Christian psychiatrists, trained in detecting purely psychological problems, acknowledge the reality of demon possession. Missionaries, evangelists, and Christian counselors have had wide experience with demon possession.

How do we know if someone is possessed versus just oppressed by a demon?

Demon *oppression* is the external influence of demons on individuals. Jesus "went about doing good and healing all who were oppressed by the devil" (Acts 10:38). Demon *possession* is the exercise of internal control over the person. This is described in several ways including "demonized" (Matt. 15:22); "with" an unclean spirit (Mark 1:23); and "have" an evil spirit (Mark 9:17). There are several characteristics of those "possessed" by demons:

1. Severe sickness (Matt. 12:22)
2. Psychic powers (Acts 16:16)
3. Unusual physical strength (Mark 5:3)
4. Fits of rage (Mark 5:4)
5. Other personalities living within (Marek 5:6–7)
6. Different voices from within (Mark 5:6–7)
7. Resistant to spiritual help (Mark 5:7)
8. Hypersensitivity (Mark 5:7)
9. Involvement in occult practices (Deut. 18:10–11)

No one of these is a necessary sign of demon possession. However, these are symptoms and therefore warning signs. If they persist, one should consult a Christian counselor trained in this area. In addition, one cannot contract this spiritual "disease" by casual contact. Demons never enter a life uninvited. He enters only disobedient hearts, for he is "the spirit that is now working in the sons of disobedience" (Eph. 2:2). One must open the door for them by:

1. Yielding to sin (John 8:14)
2. Spiritual stubbornness or rebellion (1 Sam. 15:23)

3. Occult practices such as astrology, mediums (channelers), fortune–tellers, trying to contact the dead, etc. (Deut. 18:11).

4. Transfer of occult powers (by some ritual).

These all involve free and deliberate acts. No one is forced by demons against their will. People freely invite demons into their lives by a combination of moral rebellion and occult association and practice.

How does an unbeliever escape demonic possession?

If an unbeliever is really possessed by a demon, then he or she must realize that the only cure is based on the sacrificial death of Jesus Christ (Col. 2:14–15). The first step for the unbeliever plagued by demonic possession is to trust in Jesus Christ for salvation (John 1:12; Col. 1:13). Deliverance from a demon is a biblical function and should be done only in the name of Jesus as Paul did in Acts 16:16–18 (see Acts 5:16; Matt. 10:1; Jude 9). If one places their trust in Jesus Christ as Savior, they are then protected from demonic ownership since they are eternally and securely possessed by Christ (1 Cor. 6:19–20).

When is demon activity directly involved?

Demons are involved directly or indirectly in anything that is opposed to the plan and will of God. However, the Bible identifies a number of things that are clearly the result of direct demonic activity:

1. False predictions (Deut. 18:21–22)
2. Contacting departed spirits (Deut. 18:11)
3. Using instruments of divination (Deut. 18:11a)
4. Advocating idolatry or images (Ex. 20:3–4; Deut. 13:1–3)

5. Denial of Christ's humanity or deity (Col. 2:9; 1 John 4:1–2)
6. Advocating abstinence from certain foods for religious reasons (1 Tim. 4:3–4)
7. Depreciating or denying marriage (1 Tim. 4:3)
8. Promoting immorality (Eph. 2:2–3; Jude 7)
9. Encouraging legalistic self–denial (Col. 2:16–23)
10. Denying death (Gen. 3:4)
11. Encouraging self–deification Gen. 3:5; 2 Thess. 2:9)
12. Promoting lying (John 8:44)
13. Advocating astrology (Deut. 4:19; Isa. 47:13–15)

Can Christians be demon possessed?

Demonic possession of a believer is not supported in Scripture. This is especially true given what is done on the behalf of the believer by the Holy Spirit at the moment of salvation. The believer becomes the *possession* of God through sealing (2 Cor. 1:22; Eph. 1:13–14) and the permanent indwelling (John 14:16) of the third person of the Trinity (Holy Spirit). The believer has the present and permanent possession of eternal life (John 5:24). Given this, demonic possession seems limited to unbelievers. However, demonic oppression, attack from without, is a possible reality for a believer and can be quite sever (Job 1:11; 2:5, 9; Luke 22:31–32).

What can demons (Satan) do to Christians?

The Bible lists a number of things Satan and demons can do, if permitted by God, to believers:

- Direct attack materially (Job 1:11; 2:5, 9) physically (Job 2:7–8), spiritually (Job 1:11; 2:5, 9)
- He can "sift" the Christian (Luke 22:31–32)
- He can "fill" the heart to lie (Acts 5:3–4)

- He can "destroy the flesh" (1 Cor. 5:5)
- He can "tempt" (1 Cor. 7:5; 1 Thess. 3:5)
- He can "take advantage" (2 Cor. 11:3)
- He can "corrupt" (2 Cor. 11:3)
- He can "buffet" (2 Cor. 12:7)
- He can try to "hinder" (1 Thess. 2:18)
- He wants to "trap" (1 Tim. 3:7; 2 Tim. 2:26)
- He wants to "devour" (1 Peter 5:8)
- He "accuses" (Rev. 12:10)

How does someone escape the oppression of demons?

Christians are vulnerable to demonic oppression especially through their own lusts and the enticements of the world (James 1:14–15; 1 John 2:16). Scripture gives steps to take when we are trying to free ourselves from bondage:

1. Confess our sin (1 John 1:9).
2. Renounce the works of Satan (2 Cor. 4:2).
3. Destroy occult objects, even if it involves a large financial loss (2 Chron. 14:2–5; 23:17; Acts 19:17–20).
4. Break fellowship with occultists (2 Cor. 6:14–16).
5. Resist the devil (James 4:7) and flee temptation (1 Cor. 6:18; 10:14; 1 Tim. 6:11; 2 Tim. 2:22).
6. Meditate on and apply the word of God (Eph. 6:17; Matt. 4:4, 7, 10), live in accordance with biblical truth.
7. Pray about it with other believers (Eph. 6:18; Matt. 18:19).

Struggle against the powers of darkness is real and can be overbearing. However, we have the comfort of knowing that we "overcome them; because greater is He

[God] who is in you than he [Satan] who is in the world" (1 John 4:4).

Summary

The Bible answers many of our questions about angels, Satan and demons. We must resist any urge to elevate the place of angels too high or diminish their role and reality in our world. Indeed, the Bible gives us all that we need to know and believe to live a life pleasing to God even in a world with demons. Such certainly involves a belief and correct understanding of angels, Satan and demons.

Questions to Answer

1. What are some of the most important questions about angels?
2. What is our primary basis for believing angels are real?
3. What biblical verses help us understand the most about angels?
4. What biblical verses help us identify Satan's schemes and activity in our world?
5. What biblical verses help us understand and fight spiritual warfare?

Appendix A:

Why Does God Allow Evil & Demons?

Christianity affirms the reality of evil, demons and the existence of an all perfect, transcendent God. Hence, Christianity affirms both God and evil. Often this is viewed as a contradiction. However, a contradiction is only when one affirms as true both "A" and its opposite "non-A" at the same time and the same sense. Only if we affirmed both God and no-God or evil and no-evil, would this be a contradiction. This is only an apparent inconsistency or difficulty that exits. In other words, we affirm 1. God in accordance with his all perfect nature would abolish evil and 2. Evil exists. Therefore, at some point God will abolish or defeat all evil. It is not necessary to negate God, His nature or evil. In addressing this question: there are usually three areas regarding God and evil: 1) what is the nature of evil? 2) What is the origin of evil? And 3) what is the purpose of evil?

Nature of Evil

The argument against the Christian position concerning the nature of evil is usually stated as follows:

1. God is the author of everything.
2. Evil is something.
3. Therefore, God is the author of evil.

If we reject premise 1 and say God is not the author of everything, it seems dualism would be true, that is something exists that God did not create, would be the result. If we deny premise 2 then it seems we deny the reality of evil. But if we cannot deny premise 1 or 2, the argument follows that God is the author of evil. The solution to the dilemma was offered by Augustine (354–430 AD),

> For evil has no positive nature; but loss of good has received the name 'evil' Evil is not a substance; for if it were a substance, it would be good. (*City of God*, 11.9)

Hence, evil is not a "thing" or "substance" but a lack in things. It is like rust to a car, rot to a tree, or a parasite to a host. It is the absence of good. Hence, we can correct the argument by stating:

1. God [only] created substances.
2. Evil is not a substance.
3. Therefore, God did not create evil.

It is also important to note that not every absence of good is evil. As Thomas Aquinas (1224/5–1274) said,

> But what is evil is a *privation*; in this sense blindness means the privation of sight . . . A thing is called evil for lacking a perfection it ought to have; to lack sight is evil in man, but not in a stone. (*Summa* 1.48.3).

Hence, the lack of good must be part of a things nature just as it is of the nature of a person to see, lack thereof is evil, but not so with a stone since it is not its nature to see.

ORIGIN OF EVIL

The argument against the Christian position concerning the origin of evil may be stated as follows:

1. God is absolutely perfect.
2. God cannot create anything imperfect.
3. But perfect creatures cannot do evil.
4. Therefore, evil cannot arise in such a world.

If premise 1 or 2 is wrong, then so is theism. So it must be premise 3 that is false. Perfect creatures can do evil. God made all creatures good, but some creatures became evil by free choice. Hence, God gave some creatures free will. God produces the fact of free choice; humans and angels perform the acts of free choice. God is responsible for creating the possibility of evil, but humans and angels are responsible for the actuality or reality of evil. Hence, we can offer the following correction:

1. God is absolutely perfect.
2. God created only perfect creatures.
3. One perfection God gave some creatures was free choice.
4. By free choice, these creatures brought evil.
5. Therefore, a perfect creature caused evil.

God is free but cannot do evil because He is all perfect and cannot change. Humans are free and can do evil because they can change. Angels are created free and then make their choice to obey or disobey God which, because of their nature (see Chapter 1), becomes permanent. God's creation of humans and angels produced the possibility of evil, but they preformed the acts of freedom, hence creatures make evil actual.

PURPOSE OF EVIL

Why does God allow evil? David Hume put the dilemma in its most succinct form:

> Is he willing to prevent evil, but not able? Then he is impotent. Is he able, but not willing? Then he is malevolent. Is he both able and willing? Whence then is evil? (*Dialogues Concerning Natural Religion*, Part X).

This is perhaps the most difficult question for the theist to answer. While this does not eliminate God, it has turned some to finite Godism. We can state the argument as follows:

1. If God is all–good, he would destroy evil.
2. If God is all–powerful, he could destroy evil.
3. But evil is not destroyed.
4. Therefore, there is no such God.

Since we cannot deny premise 1 and 2, the problem is with premise 3. First, to know that evil is not ever destroyed, we would have to know everything or *be* God to know the premise is true. Second, the word *destroy* is ambiguous. God could destroy evil now but would also be destroying all freedom. That would be an evil itself. Evil cannot be destroyed without destroying freedom. Love is the greatest good for free creatures, but love is impossible without freedom. So, to destroy freedom would not be the greatest good. If *destroy* is taken in a weaker form as in *defeat* such as to separate good from evil or be victorious over evil then it must be done without destroying free will. Hence, we can make the following correction:

1. God is all–good and desires to defeat evil.
2. God is all–powerful and is able to defeat evil.
3. Evil is not **yet** defeated.
4. Therefore, it will one day be defeated.

Christianity must point to the all–perfect nature of God that someday *will* defeat evil. Theologically speaking the way God will defeat evil is by quarantining people and angels who choose evil (i.e., hell).

So why did God create if he knew evil would result? The Christian must maintain that no other world achievable is morally better than the one God made where creatures are free. Hence, we can compare this world to the possible ones: God could have: 1) created no world at all. But a nonexistent world is not morally better than this one. 2. Created no world with free creatures. But a non–free world is not morally better than this one. 3) Created free creatures that would do no evil. But a moral world with no evil while logically possible is not actually attainable since some freely chose to do evil. 4) Created free creatures who would do evil but would all be saved in the end. Even if it were achievable, it would not be more desirable since the doing of evil is free and the choosing of salvation is free. This is the best achievable world, given free will. This may not be the best of all possible worlds (conceivable), but it is ultimately the best *way* to the best possible world (achievable) given the necessity of free will. God could not have done better then what he actually did.

So what about evil that seems to have no purpose? The argument may be stated as follows:

1. An all–good God must have a good purpose for everything.
2. There is no good purpose for some suffering.
3. Therefore, there cannot be an all–good God.

Here we must be reminded of our finitude. Just because we do not know a good purpose for evil, does not mean there is no good purpose. Just because finite minds can't think of an answer, does not mean an infinite mind cannot. Not every event has a specific good purpose; it may be a general good purpose. Fire or water, for example has a general good purpose. But not every spark has a good purpose such as igniting an unintended fire or water may result in drowning. Furthermore, God is able to bring much good out of unintended evils such as when a drowning victim is saved. As we have shown, this world is not the best of all possible worlds. But God has made it the best possible way to attain his ultimate goal of the greater good. An all knowing God knows everything; finite creatures do not know everything. Hence, God knows what we do not know. An all good God has a good purpose for all evil even if we do not know what it is. Given that we do know some good purposes for evil it is a reasonable inference. Having us not knowing the other good purposes may be part of God's good purposes. As C. S. Lewis said,

> God whispers to us in our pleasures, speaks in our conscience, but shouts in our pains: it is His megaphone to rouse a deaf world. (*Problem of Pain,* 81)

We can reply to the argument as follows:
1. God must have a good purpose for everything.
2. Some good purposes have evil by–products.
3. Therefore, some evil is a by–product of a good purpose.

Hence, we have shown that evil does not negate 1) the existence of God and 2) the all–perfect nature of God. In fact we should note the entire notion of objecting to God from evil should point us to God's very existence. As C. S. Lewis said,

> My argument against God was that the universe seemed so cruel and unjust. But how had I got this idea of *just* and *unjust*. A man does not call a

line crooked unless he has some idea of a straight line . . . Thus in the very act of trying to prove that God did not exist—in other words, that the whole of reality was senseless—I found I was forced to assume that one part of reality—namely my idea of justice—was full of sense. (*Mere Christianity*, 45–46)

For more on this topic see Norman L. Geisler *If God, Why Evil? A New Way to Look at the Question.*

Appendix B:

Central Bible Passages On Angels

ANGELIC VISITORS — GENESIS 18, 19

When he lifted up his eyes and looked, behold, three men were standing opposite him; and when he saw them, he ran from the tent door to meet them and bowed himself to the earth, and said, " My Lord, if now I have found favor in Your sight, please do not pass Your servant by. Please let a little water be brought and wash your feet, and rest yourselves under the tree; and I will bring a piece of bread, that you may refresh yourselves; after that you may go on, since you have visited your servant." And they said, "So do, as you have said. "So Abraham hurried into the tent to Sarah, and said, "Quickly, prepare three measures of fine flour, knead it and make bread cakes. "Abraham also ran to the herd, and took a tender and choice calf and gave it to the servant, and he hurried to prepare it. He took curds and milk and the calf which he had prepared, and placed it before them; and he was standing by them under the tree as they ate. (Gen. 18:2–8)

So they pressed hard against Lot and came near to break the door. But the men reached out their hands and brought Lot into the house with them, and shut the door. They struck the men who were at the doorway of the house with blindness, both small and great, so that they wearied themselves trying to find the doorway. (Gen. 19:9–11)

BELIEVERS' ADVANCED AGENTS – GENESIS 24:40

He said to me, 'The Lord, before whom I have walked, will send His angel with you to make your journey successful, and you will take a wife for my son from my relatives and from my father's house. (Gen. 24:40)

HEAVEN'S FOOD DELIVERY SERVICE – 1 KINGS 19

He [Elijah] lay down and slept under a juniper tree; and behold, there was an angel touching him, and he said to him, "Arise, eat. "Then he looked and behold, there was at his head a bread cake baked on hot stones, and a jar of water. So he ate and drank and lay down again. The angel of the Lord came again a second time and touched him and said, "Arise, eat, because the journey is too great for you. "So he arose and ate and drank, and went in the strength of that food forty days and forty nights to Horeb, the mountain of God. (1 Kings 19:5–8)

GOD'S INVISIBLE ARMY – 2 KINGS 6

Behold, an army with horses and chariots was circling the city. And his servant said to him, "Alas, my master! What shall we do?" So he answered, "Do not fear, for those who are with us are more than those who are with them." Then Elisha prayed and said, "O Lord, I pray, open his eyes that he may see." And the Lord opened the servant's eyes and he saw; and behold, the mountain was full of horses and chariots of fire all around Elisha. (2 Kings 6:15–17)

SPIRITUAL SENTINELS — GENESIS 3; PSALMS 80, 99

So He drove the man out; and at the east of the garden of Eden He stationed the cherubim and the flaming sword which turned every direction to guard the way to the tree of life. (Gen. 3:24)

Oh, give ear, Shepherd of Israel, You who lead Joseph like a flock; You who are enthroned above the cherubim, shine forth! (Ps. 80:1)

The Lord reigns, let the peoples tremble; He is enthroned above the cherubim, let the earth shake! The Lord is great in Zion, And He is exalted above all the peoples. (Ps. 99:1–2)

GOD'S RESCUE SQUAD — PSALM 91

For He will give His angels charge concerning you, to guard you in all your ways. They will bear you up in their hands, that you do not strike your foot against a stone. You will tread upon the lion and cobra, the young lion and the serpent you will trample down. (Ps. 91:11–13)

GOD'S REGAL ATTENDANTS — ISAIAH 6

I saw the Lord sitting on a throne, lofty and exalted, with the train of His robe filling the temple. Seraphim stood above Him, each having six wings: with two he covered his face, and with two he covered his feet, and with two he flew. And one called out to another and said,

Holy, Holy, Holy, is the Lord of hosts, The whole earth is full of His glory. (Isa. 6:1–3)

HEAVENLY PRIESTS — REVELATION 8:3

Another angel came and stood at the altar, holding a golden censer; and much incense was given to him, so that he might add it to the prayers of all the saints on the golden altar which was before the throne. (Rev. 8:3)

GUARDIANS OF GOD'S GLORY — EZEKIEL 1

Within it there were figures resembling four living beings. And this was their appearance: they had human form. Each of them had four faces and four wings. Their legs were straight and their feet were like a calf's hoof, and they gleamed like burnished bronze. Under their wings on their four sides were human hands. As for the faces and wings of the four of them, their wings touched one another; their faces did not turn when they moved, each went straight forward. As for the form of their faces, each had the face of a man; all four had the face of a lion on the right and the face of a bull on the left, and all four had the face of an eagle. Such were their faces. Their wings were spread out above; each had two touching another being, and two covering their bodies (Ezek. 5:1–11)

PROVIDENTIAL WATCHMEN — DANIEL 4:13, 23

I was looking in the visions in my mind as I lay on my bed, and behold, an angelic watcher, a holy one, descended from heaven. (Dan. 4:13)

In that the king saw an angelic watcher, a holy one, descending from heaven and saying, "Chop down the tree and destroy it; yet leave the stump with its roots in the ground, but with a band of iron and bronze around it in the new grass of the field, and let him be drenched with the dew of heaven, and let him share with the beasts of the field until seven periods of time pass over him." (Dan. 4:23)

Heavenly Postmen — Daniel 10

Then behold, a hand touched me and set me trembling on my hands and knees. He said to me, "O Daniel, man of high esteem, understand the words that I am about to tell you and stand upright, for I have now been sent to you." And when he had spoken this word to me, I stood up trembling. Then he said to me, "Do not be afraid, Daniel, for from the first day that you set your heart on understanding this and on humbling yourself before your God, your words were heard, and I have come in response to your words. (Dan. 10:10–12)

Israel's Heavenly Prime Minster — Daniel 12

Now at that time Michael, the great prince who stands guard over the sons of your people, will arise. And there will be a time of distress such as never occurred since there was a nation until that time; and at that time your people, everyone who is found written in the book, will be rescued. Many of those who sleep in the dust of the ground will awake, these to everlasting life, but the others to disgrace and everlasting contempt. Those who have insight will shine brightly like the brightness of the expanse of heaven, and those who lead the many to righteousness, like the stars forever and ever. (Dan. 12:1–3)

Heavenly Reconnaissance Agents — Zechariah 1

Then I said, "My lord, what are these?" And the angel who was speaking with me said to me, "I will show you what these are. "And the man who was standing among the myrtle trees answered and said, "These are those whom the Lord has sent to patrol the earth. "So they answered the angel of the Lord who was standing among the myrtle trees and said, "We have patrolled the earth, and behold, all the earth is peaceful and quiet." (Zech. 9–11)

BELIEVER'S BODY GUARD — MATTHEW 18:10; HEBREWS 1:14

See that you do not despise one of these little ones, for I say to you that their angels in heaven continually see the face of My Father who is in heaven. (Matt. 18:10)

Are they not all ministering spirits, sent out to render service for the sake of those who will inherit salvation? (Heb. 1:14)

HEAVENLY HARVESTERS — MATTHEW 13:24–43

And He said, "The one who sows the good seed is the Son of Man, and the field is the world; and as for the good seed, these are the sons of the kingdom; and the tares are the sons of the evil one; and the enemy who sowed them is the devil, and the harvest is the end of the age; and the reapers are angels. So just as the tares are gathered up and burned with fire, so shall it be at the end of the age. The Son of Man will send forth His angels, and they will gather out of His kingdom all stumbling blocks, and those who commit lawlessness, and will throw them into the furnace of fire; in that place there will be weeping and gnashing of teeth. (Matt. 13:37–42)

WITNESS OF OUR WILL — LUKE 12:8

And I say to you, everyone who confesses Me before men, the Son of Man will confess him also before the angels of God." (Luke 12:8)

HEAVEN'S HOSPITALITY COMMITTEE — LUKE 15:10

In the same way, I tell you, there is joy in the presence of the angels of God over one sinner who repents." (Luke 15:10)

Heavenly Escorts — Luke 16:22

Now the poor man died and was carried away by the angels to Abraham's bosom; and the rich man also died and was buried. (Luke 16:22)

Spiritual Spectators —
1 Corinthians 4:9; 1 Timothy 5:21

For, I think, God has exhibited us apostles last of all, as men condemned to death; because we have become a spectacle to the world, both to angels and to men. (1 Cor. 4:9)

I solemnly charge you in the presence of God and of Christ Jesus and of His chosen angels, to maintain these principles without bias, doing nothing in a spirit of partiality. (1 Tim. 5:21)

Heaven's Graduate Students — Ephesians 3:8–10

To me [Paul], the very least of all saints, this grace was given, to preach to the Gentiles the unfathomable riches of Christ, and to bring to light what is the administration of the mystery which for ages has been hidden in God who created all things; so that the manifold wisdom of God might now be made known through the church to the rulers and the authorities in the heavenly places. (Eph. 3:8–10)

The Celestial Choir — Revelation 4–5

And the four living creatures, each one of them having six wings, are full of eyes around and within; and day and night they do not cease to say,

Holy, holy, holy is the Lord God, the Almighty, who was and who is and who is to come. (Rev. 4:8)

Then I looked, and I heard the voice of many angels around the throne and the living creatures and the elders; and the number of them was myriads of myriads, and thousands of thousands, saying with a loud voice,

"Worthy is the Lamb that was slain to receive power and riches and wisdom and might and honor and glory and blessing." (Rev. 5:12)

WARDENS OF THE WICKED — REVELATION 9:7–11

The appearance of the locusts was like horses prepared for battle; and on their heads appeared to be crowns like gold, and their faces were like the faces of men. They had hair like the hair of women, and their teeth were like the teeth of lions. They had breastplates like breastplates of iron; and the sound of their wings was like the sound of chariots, of many horses rushing to battle. They have tails like scorpions, and stings; and in their tails is their power to hurt men for five months. They have as king over them, the angel of the abyss; his name in Hebrew is Abaddon, and in the Greek he has the name Apollyon.

COSMIC ADMINISTRATORS — REVELATION 14:18, 16:5

Then another angel, the one who has power over fire, came out from the altar; and he called with a loud voice to him who had the sharp sickle, saying, "Put in your sharp sickle and gather the clusters from the vine of the earth, because her grapes are ripe." (Rev. 14:18)

And I heard the angel of the waters saying, "Righteous are You, who are and who were, O Holy One, because You judged these things; (Rev. 16:5)

Bibliography

Abanes, Richard. *Journey into the Light: Exploring Near–Death Experiences*. Grand Rapids: Baker Book House, 1996.

Adler, Mortimer. *Angels and Us*. Touchstone, 1993.

Aquinas, Thomas. *Summa Theologica.* Translated by Fathers of the English Dominican Province. Vol. 1–5. Allen, TX: Christian Classics, 1948.

_____. *On Evil*. Edited by Jean Oesterle. South Bend: University of Notre Dame Press, 1995.

Augustine. *City of God.* New York: Random House, 1950.

Collins, James. *The Thomistic Philosophy of Angels*. Catholic University of America Press, 1947.

Augustine. *City of God.* New York: Random House, 1950.

Calvin, John. *Institutes of the Christian Religion*. 2 vols. Ed. John T. McNeill. Trans. Ford Lewis Battles. In Library of Christian Classics. Vols. 20–20. Eds. John Baillie, John T. McNeill, and Henry P. Van Dusen. Philadelphia: Westminster, 1960.

Dickason, Fred C. *Angels: Elect and Evil*. Chicago: Moody Press, 1975.

Geisler, Norman L. & Douglas E. Potter. *A Popular Survey of Bible Doctrine*, NGIM, 2015.

_____. *A Prolegomena to Evangelical Theology*. NGIM, 2016.

_____. *The Bible: Its Origin, Nature & Collection, NGIM Guide to Bible Doctrine, Vol. 1*, NGIM, 2016.

_____. *The Doctrine of Christ, NGIM Guide to Bible Doctrine, Vol. 3*, NGIM, 2016.

_____. *The Doctrine of Creation, NGIM Guide to Bible Doctrine, Vol. 4*, NGIM, 2016.

_____. *The Doctrine of God, NGIM Guide to Bible Doctrine, Vol. 2*, NGIM, 2016.

Geisler, Norman L. & William C. Roach. *Defending Inerrancy*. Grand Rapids: Baker, 2011.

Geisler, Norman L. & William E. Nix. *From God to Us*. Rev. & Exp. Chicago: Moody Press, 2012.

Geisler, Norman L. *Beware of Philosophy: A Warning to Biblical Scholars*. Bastion Books, 2012.

_____. *Chosen But Free*. 3rd ed. Minneapolis: Bethany, 2010.

_____. *Creating God in the Image of Man?* Minneapolis: Bethany House, 1997.

_____. *Knowing the Truth About Creation*. Ann Arbor: Servant Books, 1989.

_____. *Miracles and the Modern Mind*, rev. 2nd ed. Bastion Books, 2012.

_____. *Signs and Wonders*. Wheaton: Tyndale House, 1988.

_____. *Systematic Theology*. Minneapolis: Bethany, 2011.

_____. *The Big Book of Christian Apologetics*. Baker Books, 2012

_____. *Twelve Points That Show Christianity is True*. Bastion Books, 2012.

Hume, David. *Dialogues Concerning Natural Religion*. Indianapolis, Bobbs-Merrill, 1962.

Ice, Thomas & Robert Dean, Jr. *A Holy Rebellion: Strategy for Spiritual Warfare*. Harvest House, 1990.

Koch, Kurt E. *Christian Counseling and Occultism*. Grand Rapids: Kregel, 1972.

_____. *Occult Bondage and Deliverance*. Grand Rapids: Kregel, 1976.

Kole, Andre, & Al Janssen. *Miracles or Magic?* Eugene: Harvest House, 1984.

Korem, Danny, & Paul Meier. *Powers: Testing the Psychic and Supernatural*. Downers Grove: InterVarsi, 1988.

Lewis, C. S. *Mere Christianity*. New York: Macmillan, 1943.

_____. *Miracles*. New York: Macmillan, 1947.

_____. *The Abolition of Man*. New York: Macmillan, 1947.

_____. *The Problem of Pain*, New York: Macmillan, 1940.

_____. *Screwtape Letters. New York: Macmillan, 1961.*

Rhodes, Ron. *Angels Among Us: Separating Truth From Fiction*. Oregon: Harvest House, 1994.

_____. *Christ Before the Manger: The Life and Times of the Preincarnate Christ*. Grand Rapids, Baker, 1992.

Schaff, Philip. *A Select Library of the Nicene and Post–Nicene Fathers of the Christian Church*. Grand Rapids: Eerdmans, 1988–1991.

Unger, Merrill. *Biblical Demonology. Wheaton: Van Kampen, 1952.*

Walvoord, John, & Roy Zuck, eds. *The Bible Knowledge Commentary.* Vols. 1–2. Wheaton: Victor, 1987.

NORM GEISLER INTERNATIONAL MINISTRIES

Norm Geisler International Ministries is dedicated to carrying on the life's work of its co-founder, Norman L. Geisler. Described as a cross between Billy Graham and Thomas Aquinas, Norm Geisler, PhD, is a prolific author, professor, apologist, philosopher, and theologian. He has authored or co-authored over 100 books and co-founded 2 seminaries.

NGIM is focused on equipping others to proclaim and defend the Christian Faith by providing evangelism and apologetic training.

More Information

Website:	http://NormGeisler.com
Training:	http://NGIM.org (Norm Geisler International Ministries)
e–Books:	http://BastionBooks.com
Email:	Dr.NormanGeisler@outlook.com
Facebook:	http://facebook.com/normgeisler
Twitter:	https://www.twitter.com/normgeisler
Videos:	http://www.youtube.com/user/DrNormanLGeisler/videos
Biblical Inerrancy:	http://DefendingInerrancy.com
Seminaries:	Southern Evangelical Seminary http://SES.edu
	Veritas Evangelical Seminary http://VES.edu

Other books from

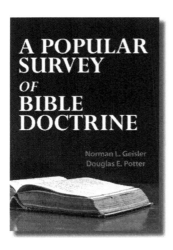

CHRISTIANS, more than ever, need a basic introduction to Bible doctrine that is systematic and true to Scripture. This book is a popular introduction to the study of Bible doctrine firmly in the evangelical tradition. Each chapter covers a biblical doctrine, stresses its doctrinal importance and inter-connectedness to formulating a Christian world view. The study questions provided help reinforce the material and make it usable even for a formal study of Bible doctrine. It is ideal for personal study and in groups for the home, church, school or ministry environment.

www.NGIM.org

NGIM
Guide to
Bible Doctrine

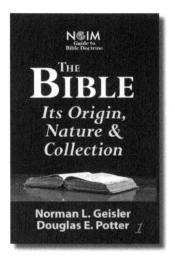

NGIM Guide to Bible Doctrine Book 1

THIS is a popular introduction to the study of the doctrine of the Bible firmly rooted in the evangelical tradition. Each chapter covers an area of the doctrine of the Bible, stresses its basis, doctrinal importance and interconnectedness to formulating a Christian view of the Bible and other doctrines. The study questions provided help reinforce the material and make it usable even for a formal study of the Bible's nature. It is ideal for personal study or in groups for the home, church, school or ministry environment.

www.NGIM.org

N⬤IM
Bible Doctrine

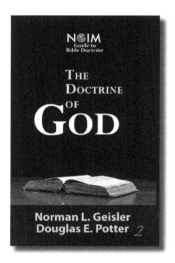

NGIM Guide to Bible Doctrine Book 2

This is a popular introduction to the study of the biblical doctrine of God firmly in the evangelical tradition. Each chapter covers an area of the doctrine of God, stresses its biblical basis, doctrinal importance and interconnectedness to formulating a Christian view of God. The study questions provided help reinforce the material and make it usable even for a formal study of God's nature. It is ideal for personal study or in groups for the home, church, school or ministry environment.

www.NGIM.org

Manufactured by Amazon.ca
Bolton, ON

31087252R00059